pathfinder® *guide*

Shakespeare Country, Vale of Evesham *and the* Cotswolds

WALKS

Compiled by
Brian Conduit

JARROLD
publishing

D0227530

Acknowledgements
My thanks for the assistance I have received from the following Countryside
Access and Rights of Way officers:
M. Overbeke and Mrs J. Harris (Warwickshire County Council) and L.H.
Chambers (Hereford and Worcester County Council). Also thanks to the
licensees of The Village at Barnsley and the Swan Inn at Islip for permission
to use their car parks.

Text:	Brian Conduit
	Revised text for 2005 edition,
	Terry Marsh
Photography:	Brian Conduit
Editorial:	Ark Creative, Norwich
Design:	Ark Creative, Norwich
Mapping:	Heather Pearson, Tina Shaw
Series Consultant:	Brian Conduit

Jarrold Publishing   ISBN 0-7117-0994-7

While every care has been taken to ensure the accuracy of the route
directions, the publishers cannot accept responsibility for errors or
omissions, or for changes in details given. The countryside is not static:
hedges and fences can be removed, field boundaries can alter, footpaths can
be rerouted and changes in ownership can result in the closure or diversion
of some concessionary paths. Also, paths that are easy and pleasant for
walking in fine conditions may become slippery, muddy and difficult in wet
weather, while stepping stones across rivers and streams may become
impassable.
    If you find an inaccuracy in either the text or maps, please write to or
e-mail Jarrold Publishing at the addresses below.

First published 1998
by Jarrold Publishing and Ordnance Survey
Revised and reprinted 2005.

Printed in Singapore. 2/05
by Craft Print International Limited

Jarrold Publishing,
Pathfinder Guides, Whitefriars, Norwich NR3 1JR
email: info@totalwalking.co.uk
www.totalwalking.co.uk

Front cover: The River Windrush at Bourton-on-the-Water
Previous page: Tewkesbury Abbey

Contents

The National Trust; The Ramblers' Association; Walkers and the Law; Countryside Access Charter; Walking Safety; Useful Organisations; Ordnance Survey Maps

■ Short, easy walks

■ Walks of modest length, likely to involve some modest uphill walking

■ More challenging walks which may be longer and/or over more rugged terrain, often with some stiff climbs

SCALE 1:333 333 or 1 INCH to about 5¼ MILES 1CM to 3.3KM

0 2 4 6 8   10 KILOMETRES   15

0   2   4   6   MILES 8   10

KEYMAP HEIGHTS SHOWN IN FEET

Walk	Page	Start	Nat. Grid Reference	Distance	Time	Highest Point
Alcester and Coughton Court	44	Alcester	SP 091575	6 miles (9.7km)	3 hrs	246ft (75m)
Aston Cantlow and Wilmcote	47	Aston Cantlow	SP 139599	6½ miles (10.5km)	3 hrs	278ft (85m)
Barnsley Park and the Coln Valley	50	Barnsley	SP 076051	6½ miles (10.5km)	3½ hrs	501ft (153m)
The Barringtons and Windrush	39	Great Barrington	SP 207136	5½ miles (8.9km)	2½ hrs	551ft (168m)
Bledington, Westcote and Icomb	53	Bledington	SP 244228	7 miles (11.3km)	3½ hrs	633ft (193m)
Bourton-on-the-Water and the Rissingtons	36	Bourton-on-the-Water	SP 167208	5½ miles (8.9km)	3 hrs	580ft (177m)
Brailes Hill	29	Lower Brailes	SP 315393	5 miles (8km)	2½ hrs	590ft (180m)
Bretforton and Honeybourne	59	Bretforton	SP 093438	7½ miles (12.1km)	3½ hrs	213ft (65m)
Broadway and Buckland	22	Broadway	SP 094375	4½ miles (7.2km)	2 hrs	570ft (174m)
Burton Dassett Hills and the surrounding villages	86	Burton Dassett Hills Country Park	SP 395521	8½ miles (13.7km)	4½ hrs	643ft (196m)
Cold Aston, Notgrove and Turkdean	65	Cold Aston	SP 129197	7 miles (11.3km)	3½ hrs	761ft (232m)
Edge Hill	32	Radway	SP 372483	4½ miles (7.2km)	2½ hrs	656ft (200m)
Elmley Castle and the Combertons	56	Elmley Castle	SO 984411	7 miles (11.3km)	3½ hrs	229ft (70m)
Evesham and the River Avon	20	Evesham	SP 037438	5½ miles (8.9km)	2½ hrs	200ft (61m)
Fairford	14	Fairford	SP 152012	3 miles (4.8km)	1½ hrs	262ft (80m)
Hay Wood, Rowington and Baddesley Clinton	78	Hay Wood car park	SP 215707	8 miles (12.9km)	4 hrs	416ft (127m)
Ilmington and Ebrington	68	Ilmington	SP 211434	7 miles (11.3km)	3½ hrs	853ft (260m)
Mickleton and the Hidcotes	34	Mickleton	SP 161437	4½ miles (7.2km)	2½ hrs	574ft (175m)
Moreton-in-Marsh and Batsford	16	Moreton-in-Marsh	SP 205325	4½ miles (7.2km)	2 hrs	590ft (180m)
Otmoor	42	Islip	SP 528139	6½ miles (10.5km)	3 hrs	285ft (87m)
Stratford-upon-Avon and the Stour Valley	82	Stratford-upon-Avon	SP 204548	9 miles (14.5km)	4½ hrs	265ft (81m)
Tewkesbury	12	Tewkesbury	SO 893324	3½ miles (5.6km)	1½ hrs	50ft (15m)
Upton and the River Severn	24	Upton upon Severn	SO 851407	5½ miles (8.9km)	2½ hrs	52ft (16m)
Warwick and the Grand Union Canal	71	Warwick, Market Place	SP 280649	8½ miles (13.7km)	4½ hrs	360ft (110m)
Welcombe Hills and Snitterfield	62	Welcombe Hills car park	SP 215573	7 miles (11.3km)	3½ hrs	360ft (110m)
Welford-on-Avon, Barton and Dorsington	75	Welford-on-Avon	SP 149518	8 miles (12.9km)	4 hrs	180ft (55m)
Wellesbourne, Hampton Lucy and Charlecote Park	26	Wellesbourne, near church	SP 278556	5½ miles (8.9km)	2½ hrs	141ft (43m)
Wroxton and Drayton	18	Wroxton	SP 414418	4 miles (6.4km)	2 hrs	508ft (155m)

Comments

A pleasant walk in the Arden countryside, passing an historic house connected with the Gunpowder Plot. Much of the return leg is beside the River Arrow.

The walk links the village in which Shakespeare's parents were married with his mother's childhood home, and includes an attractive stretch of canal.

You proceed across Barnsley Park, with a view of the great house, to the Coln valley and an enjoyable stretch of riverside walking.

Fine views over the Windrush valley are followed by pleasant walking close to or beside the river, taking in the three attractive villages of Windrush, Great Barrington and Little Barrington.

A pleasant walk in the quiet and gentle countryside of the Evenlode valley, passing through four villages.

Two quiet villages are passed through and there are attractive views over pools created from former gravel workings on this walk to the east of bustling Bourton-on-the-Water.

From the gentle slopes of Brailes Hill there are extensive views across the countryside of south Warwickshire.

A lengthy but easy walk across the Vale of Evesham below the Cotswold escarpment, linking two interesting villages.

A pleasant walk over wooded hills, partly on the Cotswold Way, links the popular village of Broadway with the quiet village of Buckland.

There are beautiful stone villages, medieval churches, an 18th-century hall and extensive views from the slopes of the Burton Dassett Hills.

There are grand views over lonely wold country on this walk which links three of the less well-known, but highly attractive, Cotswold villages.

After climbing up to the ridge of Edge Hill, you continue along it through delightful woodland before descending back to the start.

Thatched villages with medieval churches and wide views across the vale are the chief ingredients of this walk in the Vale of Evesham in the shadow of Bredon Hill.

The majority of this walk is either beside or just above the River Avon through the Vale of Evesham, and the route also takes in the remains of Evesham Abbey.

The highlights of this route are pleasant walking beside the River Coln and visiting one of the finest Cotswold wool churches.

Parkland and woodland, field paths and a canal towpath, medieval churches and a moated manor house – all this makes up a most absorbing and varied walk.

Although the route climbs to the highest point in Warwickshire, all the ascents and descents are gentle and gradual.

Quite a steep climb on to the Cotswold escarpment rewards you with grand views over the Vale of Evesham. The walk can be combined with a visit to two gardens.

A flat, easy and attractive route, beginning in the busy town of Moreton-in-Marsh and offering the opportunity to explore Batsford Arboretum.

This walk takes you across part of the 'fen country' of Otmoor, a flat, unusual and rather secretive landscape of drained marshland.

The walk starts by the River Avon in the heart of Shakespeare Country and explores some of the quiet villages of the tributary Stour valley.

The tower of the abbey is in sight for much of this interesting circuit around Tewkesbury, part of which follows a waymarked 'Battle Trail'.

On the return leg to Upton upon Severn you follow an attractive path, part of the Severn Way, across riverside meadows.

The first part of the walk is along the towpath of the Grand Union Canal; towards the end come fine views over Warwick.

From the hills there are fine views across the Avon valley to the Cotswolds and pleasant walking along one of the most attractive stretches of the river.

Welford-on-Avon is an exceptionally pretty village and the first part of the walk is through woodland and across meadows beside the river.

Plenty of variety on a walk that takes in three villages, an attractive stretch of river, a deer park and the chance to visit a Tudor house.

Wroxton is a most attractive village and on the first part of the walk there are views across parkland to the great house of Wroxton Abbey.

At-a-glance...

Introduction to Shakespeare Country, the Vale of Evesham and the Cotswolds

More than perhaps any other part of the country, the area covered by this walking guide encompasses all the features that are generally considered to be the most traditional in the English landscape. This is an area of modest, gently rolling hills, wide and verdant river valleys, wooded tracts, small market towns and, above all, an abundance of exceptionally attractive villages – mainly timber-framed and built of brick in Shakespeare Country and the Vale of Evesham, stone-built in the Cotswolds – with most of them possessing thatched cottages, medieval churches and appealing old pubs.

The south Midlands is a convenient, if rather imprecise, name for the area. It takes in what is generally described as the Shakespeare Country of the Forest of Arden and Avon valley in Warwickshire, just to the south of Birmingham, and extends westwards along the Avon into the Vale of Evesham, reaching as far as the River Severn. To the south of the Avon is the long line of the Cotswolds, and this book includes the northern and central parts of those hills, extending roughly as far south as Cirencester and Oxford.

Shakespeare Country

The River Avon is the chief focal point of Shakespeare Country, winding its way through a landscape that is the very essence of middle England; a broad, fertile valley studded with thatched black and white villages, landscaped parklands and Tudor manor houses. During its journey it flows through the two main towns of the area, Warwick and Shakespeare's home town of Stratford-upon-Avon. William Shakespeare is one of those few people sufficiently famous to have a part of the country named after him and his presence is felt throughout the region, especially in and around Stratford. In the town centre is the house where he was born in 1564, the foundations of the house where he died in 1616, and the church in which he is buried. Nearby in the village of Shottery is the childhood home of his wife, Anne Hathaway, and in Wilmcote is the house in which Mary Arden, his mother, lived before her marriage. A little farther away in Aston Cantlow is the church in which his parents were married and at Charlecote, just to the east of Stratford, is the deer park in which he is alleged to have been caught poaching as a youth. All these places attract huge numbers of 'literary pilgrims'.

To the north of the Avon lies the Forest of Arden, also very much part of Shakespeare Country and the setting for *As You Like It*. Traditionally,

Buckland's medieval parish church

Warwickshire was always divided into the Feldon or field land to the south of the Avon, and the Arden or woodland to the north. In the Middle Ages this was an area of thick woodland and rough heathland and although it has now largely disappeared, cut down in previous centuries to feed the iron industries of Birmingham and the Black Country, it is still a well-wooded area with a number of quiet and unspoilt villages and some attractive old manor houses.

The Cotswolds penetrate into the Feldon of south Warwickshire, and not only is the terrain here hillier than in the rest of the county, but the villages are mainly built of the local limestone. This was a richer area than Arden, the churches are larger and finer and, like those in the main part of the Cotswolds, were largely financed from the profits of the wool trade.

Vale of Evesham

From Shakespeare Country the Avon continues westwards into Worcestershire and the broad expanses of the Vale of Evesham, continuing through the vale to join the Severn at Tewkesbury. This is a land of market gardens and orchards – unfortunately not as many of the latter as there used to be – noted for fruit and vegetable growing.

The chief town of the region is Evesham, where only the detached bell tower remains of its once powerful medieval abbey. Farther down the river, the east end and tower of Pershore Abbey survive, and at the confluence of the Avon and Severn, the abbey church of Tewkesbury is the best preserved of all, completing the trio of former monastic houses in the area.

The terrain of the vale is mainly flat, but the expansive views across it extend westwards to the line of the Malverns and southwards to the Cotswolds – nowhere do you feel far from the latter. The villages, as pretty as those elsewhere throughout this region, still contain plenty of thatched black and white cottages but are often stone-built, making the vale a kind of transitional zone between the Midlands and the Cotswolds.

The Cotswolds

The Cotswolds are part of a chain of oolitic limestone uplands that stretches in a roughly north east to south west direction from Yorkshire to Dorset. Unlike the carboniferous limestone of the Yorkshire Dales and Mendips, oolitic limestone does not create deep gorges and underground cave systems but a more intimate and less dramatic landscape characterised by rolling hills and gentle valleys. The Cotswolds tilt slightly to the south east, thereby thrusting up a bold and often steep escarpment on their western edge. From this escarpment a succession of fine viewpoints look westwards over the vales of Evesham and the Severn.

Behind the escarpment lies the long 'dip' slope. Here is the typical rolling wold country which drops gently down to the former royal hunting ground of Wychwood Forest and merges almost imperceptibly into the flat country of the Oxford Plain. A number of rivers with delightful-sounding names – Evenlode, Windrush, Coln – have cut wide valleys through the wolds, flowing south-eastwards into the plain to join the Thames, itself a Cotswold river in its origins.

The attractiveness of the towns and villages of the Cotswolds is legendary, and one of the most important factors in this is the local stone, which makes excellent building material. Of course the stone was only the raw material, it was the money generated by the wool trade that produced the fine churches, manor houses and other buildings for which the Cotswolds are famed. Sheep farming began with the first human inhabitants of the region, but it was the monastic foundations (at Cirencester, Winchcombe, Hailes)

The River Ray at Otmoor

that helped to pioneer the development of the wool trade, which reached its peak between the 14th and 17th centuries. At first the raw wool was exported to the continent, but in the early 14th century Edward III imported weavers from Flanders to develop a native cloth industry. By the end of the Middle Ages wool had become England's major export industry and half of it

Grazing pasture near Moreton-in-Marsh

was produced in the Cotswolds, where the advantages of an abundance of sheep, water power and good communications ensured the predominance of the region.

It is from this heyday of the cloth trade that the great architectural legacy of the Cotswolds chiefly dates. Particularly outstanding are the magnificent 15th-century 'wool churches' endowed by wealthy cloth magnates. All visitors will have their favourites, but probably the most impressive are those that rise above Cirencester, Winchcombe, Burford, Chipping Campden, Northleach and Fairford.

Walking in the area

Given the nature of the terrain, there are no really difficult or challenging walks in this guide. This is a region not of dramatic vistas but of an intimate and largely man-made landscape. There are a few steep ascents in the Cotswolds, mainly in order to reach the escarpment, but nothing too strenuous. The only real challenge in some of the walks comes from their length, not from the difficulty of the terrain.

In parts of the region, particularly in the arable country of the Vale of Evesham, some of the lesser-used footpaths may get overgrown with brambles and nettles during the summer. Apart from the inevitable muddy conditions after a rainy spell, this is likely to be the most serious problem.

While walking in Shakespeare Country, Vale of Evesham and the Cotswolds, you will be experiencing a largely traditional and unspoilt piece of England, and nowhere are you likely to be far from a pleasant market town, village pub or tearoom where you can relax and take refreshment – a pleasant accompaniment and fitting finale to any walk.

Tewkesbury

Start	Tewkesbury
Distance	3½ miles (5.6km)
Approximate time	1½ hours
Parking	Tewkesbury, Vineyards car park
Refreshments	Pubs and cafés at Tewkesbury
Ordnance Survey maps	Landranger 150 (Worcester & The Malverns), Explorer 190 (Malvern Hills & Bredon Hill)

Much of this short walk follows a waymarked 'Battle Trail' that guides you around the site of the Battle of Tewkesbury, fought in 1471. Although the route is never far from the town and rarely out of sight of buildings, this is a most attractive and absorbing walk with constantly changing views of Tewkesbury's imposing abbey and pleasant walking across meadows and beside both the rivers Avon and Severn, which meet near the end of the walk.

Tewkesbury stands near the confluence of the rivers Severn and Avon and has a wealth of fine old brick and timber-framed buildings dating from the 17th and 18th centuries. Pride of place inevitably goes to the 12th-century Benedictine abbey, one of the most outstanding Norman churches in England. Externally it is particularly noted for the tall recessed arch on the west front and the impressive central tower. Inside, the Norman pillars of the nave support a superb, vaulted, 14th-century roof, and there are some splendid tombs and monuments. Although the monastic buildings have disappeared, the great church fortunately survived Henry VIII's dissolution in the 1530s as it was bought by the local townspeople for use as a parish church.

At the car park entrance turn left, go through a metal gate and take a tarmac path across a recreation ground. Later the path becomes enclosed and continues along the left edge of a cemetery to a road Ⓐ. Turn right and at a T-junction, turn right again along the main road.

At public footpath and Battle Trail signs, turn left over a stile and walk along the right edge of a field. Just before the field corner, turn right over a stile Ⓑ, walk along a tarmac path, turn left to cross a footbridge over a brook and turn right along the right edge of a field. Bear left to head across this narrow field, climb an almost hidden stile in the far corner and turn right up to a road (Lincoln Green Lane). Turn right, then turn left through a kissing-gate into Bloody Meadow. In front is an information board about the Battle of Tewkesbury, fought on these meadows in 1471 and one of the most decisive encounters of the Wars of the Roses. The Yorkist army, led by Edward IV, routed the Lancastrians, under Margaret of Anjou, wife of the deposed and imprisoned Henry VI. As a result of his

Tewkesbury from Severn Ham

Severn and Mill Avon. As you walk along the grassy path across it there are fine views of the outline of the Malverns on the horizon. On reaching the banks of the broad River Severn, turn right **E** along a riverside path which eventually bears right away from the river – over to the left is the confluence of the Avon and Severn – to the Mill Avon again.

Go through a metal gate, cross a footbridge over the river and keep ahead to the main street in the centre of Tewkesbury **F**. Turn right to a junction by the war memorial, briefly turn right along Church Street, then turn left under an arch and along Lilleys Alley to emerge on to a road. Turn left, turn right to cross a footbridge over a stream and continue along a tarmac path. Turn right along another tarmac path enclosed between fences, alongside a cricket field and the Vineyards car park, to return to the start.　●

victory, Edward IV's position on the throne was much more secure and he ordered the execution of Henry VI and the imprisonment of Margaret of Anjou.

Keep along the right edge of Bloody Meadow, where some of the fiercest fighting took place, and at the end continue between bushes to a stile. Climb it, walk through a narrow belt of trees to a lane **C** and turn right along it to rejoin the main road. Turn left, passing a car park on the left, then turn left into the car park **D** and, just beyond the toilet block, turn right on to a tarmac path, signposted 'River', which leads to a picturesque mill building by the Mill Avon, now a restaurant.

Turn left beside the mill, cross a footbridge over the river above a weir and go through a metal gate. Ahead is Severn Ham, a delightful area of uncultivated meadow land, full of buttercups, that lies between the

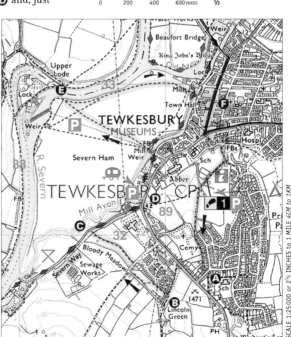

Fairford

Start	Fairford
Distance	3 miles (4.8km)
Approximate time	1½ hours
Parking	Fairford
Refreshments	Pubs and restaurants at Fairford
Ordnance Survey maps	Landranger 163 (Cheltenham & Cirencester), Explorers 169 (Cirencester & Swindon) and OL45 (The Cotswolds)

This short walk in the Coln valley, which starts by one of the grandest of the Cotswold 'wool churches', takes you round some of the pools to the east of Fairford which were created from old gravel workings and are now an attractive feature of the landscape. The finale is a delightful stroll by the River Coln.

The number of fine old inns in the town centre is an indication of Fairford's former importance on one of the main stage coach routes between London and Gloucester. Presiding over the town is the massive central tower of the parish church of St Mary, one of the finest of the Cotswold wool churches, built in the latter part of the 15th century by John Tame, a local wealthy wool merchant who is buried in the church that he and his son Edmund financed. The imposing and well-proportioned interior is

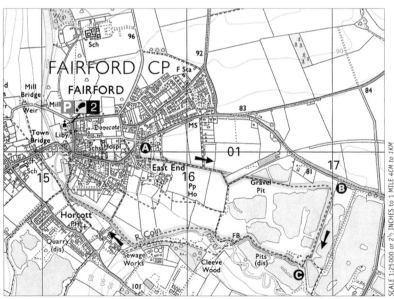

The River Coln near Fairford

particularly noted for its stained glass windows, possibly the most complete set of late medieval glass in a parish church anywhere in England.

Start at the top end of High Street by the church, walk along High Street, through the market place and turn left along London Street, in the Lechlade direction. Just after the road curves left, turn right along East End and take the first turning on the left (Beaumoor Place). At a right bend, keep ahead along a tarmac path **A**, passing to the left of a house, to a kissing-gate.

Go through the gate and now follow a path, alternately by the left edge of meadows and enclosed between trees, to reach a meadow beside one of the pools formed by gravel extraction.

Keep ahead across the meadow, drawing closer to the edge of the water, and at the end follow the path to the right **B** across the end of the pool. More pools can be seen through the trees to the left. At the next corner, do not follow the edge of the water to the

right but keep ahead to a waymarked post in front of woodland **C**. Turn right along a path that keeps by the edge of this woodland, sometimes close to the water, eventually turning left to cross a footbridge over a channel on to the banks of the River Coln.

Now comes a most attractive part of the walk as you turn right to walk along a riverside path, with wonderful views across the meadows to the right to Fairford, dominated inevitably by St Mary's church tower. Follow the river around a right curve, go through a kissing-gate in a line of trees and after going through another gate you reach Dilly's Bridge, a wooden footbridge over the river constructed in memory of a golden retriever.

Do not cross the bridge but continue along the path which bears slightly right away from the river to reach the edge of Fairford. Keep ahead along a tarmac path to a T-junction, turn left and follow the track as it curves right to emerge in the market place. Retrace your steps along High Street to return to the start. ●

Moreton-in-Marsh and Batsford

Start	Moreton-in-Marsh
Distance	4½ miles (7.2km)
Approximate time	2 hours
Parking	Moreton-in-Marsh
Refreshments	Pubs and cafés at Moreton-in-Marsh, tearoom at Batsford Arboretum
Ordnance Survey maps	Landranger 151 (Stratford-upon-Avon), Explorer OL45 (The Cotswolds)

This is a short and easy walk, of wide and expansive views, through the lush and gentle countryside that lies between Moreton-in-Marsh and the estate village of Batsford. Approximately two-thirds of the way round there is an opportunity to make a short detour to the very interesting Batsford Arboretum.

The wide and spacious main street of Moreton-in-Marsh and the number of old coaching inns is an indication of the town's former significance, lying at the junction of two major cross-country routes: the Foss Way between the Midlands and South West, and the main road from London and Oxford to Worcester and on to Wales. It is still a busy and bustling little town with a good variety of eating places. The handsome church, which lies just off the main street, is mostly Victorian.

🥾 Start by the 19th-century Town Hall and walk northwards along the main street. At a public footpath sign turn left **Ⓐ** down steps and walk across a park to a line of trees. Turn right along a grassy path between an avenue of trees, go through a gate, cross a lane, go through a kissing-gate opposite and bear slightly left across a field to go through another kissing-gate. Walk along the left edge of a field, go through a metal gate and continue along the right edge of the next field. Go through another metal gate and walk along a track, passing to the left of Dorn Priory Farm, to reach a lane in the hamlet of Dorn **Ⓑ**.

Moreton-in-Marsh

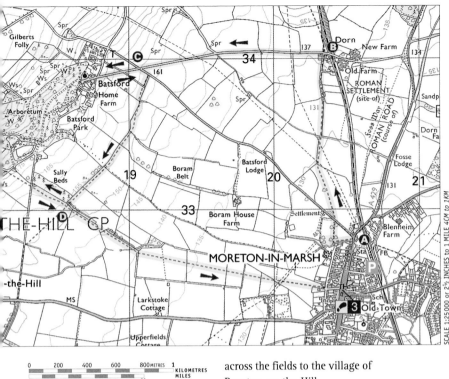

SCALE 1:25000 or 2½ INCHES to 1 MILE 4CM to 1KM

```
0    200   400   600   800 METRES  1
                                   KILOMETRES
                                   MILES
0    200   400   600 YARDS  ½
```

across the fields to the village of Bourton-on-the-Hill.

If you wish to visit Batsford Arboretum, turn right along the field edge and go through a gate on to a drive by a lodge. The arboretum was created in the 1880s by Lord Redesdale and has a large number of oriental, especially Japanese, specimens. There is also a falconry centre, garden centre and tearooms.

At the crossroads of paths, the main route continues to the left along the field edge. Go through a kissing-gate just to the right of the field corner and continue in a more or less straight line, through a succession of fields, via a series of metal kissing-gates, finally heading diagonally across a narrow field to a kissing-gate on its left edge.

Turn right across the next field, heading directly towards the buildings of Moreton-in-Marsh, and on the far side go through the last in the series of metal gates. Walk along an enclosed path to a road and keep ahead along Corders Lane to the start.

Turn left and keep along this straight, narrow and quiet lane for ¾ mile (1.2km) to a crossroads **C**. Keep ahead for a short detour into the estate village of Batsford, dominated by its imposing, neo-Norman, 19th-century church.

Return to the crossroads **C**, turn right and after 50 yds (46m), turn right again over a stile. Walk along an enclosed path, climb a stile, continue along a narrower path – which might be overgrown in places – climb another stile and a few yards ahead turn left over another one. Bear right to keep along the right edge of a succession of fields and over several stiles alongside the boundary wall of Batsford Park. Over to the right are fine views across the parkland to the late19th-century house built in the Tudor style. Eventually you cross a footbridge in a field corner and keep ahead through a gate to a crossroads of paths **D**. From here there is a very good view ahead

Wroxton and Drayton

Start	Wroxton
Distance	4 miles (6.4km)
Approximate time	2 hours
Parking	Wroxton, in Main Street near the duck pond
Refreshments	Pubs at Wroxton, pub at Drayton
Ordnance Survey maps	Landranger 151 (Stratford-upon-Avon), Explorers 191 (Banbury, Bicester & Chipping Norton) and 206 (Edge Hill & Fenny Compton)

From the idyllic village of Wroxton, the route heads first across part of the parkland of Wroxton Abbey and then continues across fields to Drayton. A disused railway track followed by quiet country lanes provide easy and relaxing walking back to the starting point.

Even in an area renowned for its villages, Wroxton ranks as an exceptionally pretty one, with a large duck pond and many thatched cottages built of the warm looking, orange-coloured ironstone found in the Oxfordshire Cotswolds. The mainly 14th-century Church of All Saints has a west tower built in 1748. Inside are

The duck pond, Wroxton

tombs of the various owners of Wroxton Abbey, including a monument to Lord North, Prime Minister at the time of the American War of Independence. It is somewhat ironic that the abbey, an imposing 17th-century mansion built on the site of a medieval priory, now serves as an annexe of an American university.

🖊 The walk starts by the duck pond in Main Street. With your back to the

pond, head towards the entrance of Wroxton College (or Abbey) and take the lane to the right of it. Where the lane bears right, turn left, at a public footpath sign to Banbury, along a path enclosed between an iron fence on the left and hedge on the right. Go through a kissing-gate, turn left and follow a grassy path across the park, keeping roughly parallel with a wire fence on the left and making for another kissing-gate. From here are fine views of Wroxton Abbey. Go through the gate, bear left downhill across a field and in the bottom corner continue across a causeway between two lakes. Climb a stile, head uphill to climb another and continue across the next field, passing an obelisk to Frederick, Prince of Wales, son of George III. Descend to cross a footbridge over a brook, keep ahead for a few yards along a track and then bear left off it **A** to pick up a clear and obvious field path.

The path initially keeps parallel to the edge of woodland on the left and continues to a stile. Climb it, cross a track, keep ahead to climb another stile and walk across a field, passing to the left of Drayton's 14th-century church. The church has quite an unusual appearance as the west tower, built in 1808, is only marginally higher than the roof of the nave. Climb a stile, continue uphill across the next field and in the far right-hand corner climb a stile on to a tarmac drive. Bear left to a road, turn left **B** and where the road bends left by the pub, keep ahead

along Queens Crescent. Where this ends, continue along a track, at a public bridleway sign, pass beside a metal gate and turn left along a tree-lined track **C**, part of a disused railway.

Follow this track, which later narrows to a path, for just over ³⁄₄ mile (1.2km) to a lane **D**. Turn left, at a T-junction turn left again **E**, in the Wroxton direction, and take the first turning on the left **F**. This narrow lane bears right to the main road on the edge of Wroxton. Keep ahead along Silver Street and where the road bends right, continue ahead along picturesque Church Street, passing in front of the church. At a T-junction, turn right to return to the start.

| 0 | 200 | 400 | 600 | 800 METRES | 1 |
| 0 | 200 | 400 | 600 YARDS | ½ | KILOMETRES / MILES |

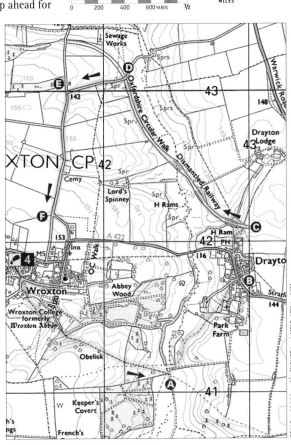

SCALE 1:25000 or 2½ INCHES to 1 MILE 4CM to 1KM

Evesham and the River Avon

Start	Evesham
Distance	5½ miles (8.9km)
Approximate time	2½ hours
Parking	Evesham. Alternatively, park at Twyford Country Centre and start the walk from there, following directions from point **D**
Refreshments	Pubs and cafés at Evesham, café at Twyford Country Centre
Ordnance Survey maps	Landranger 150 (Worcester & The Malverns), Explorer 205 (Stratford-upon-Avon & Evesham)

There is attractive walking beside the River Avon and pleasant views on this generally flat and easy stroll in the heart of the Vale of Evesham between Evesham and Twyford Country Centre. The outward route is just above the river; the almost parallel return leg hugs the riverbank all the way.

The imposing Perpendicular bell-tower of the now largely vanished abbey dominates Evesham. Other monastic survivals are the half-timbered gateway and the 14th-century Almonry, formerly the home of the abbey almoner and now a tourist information and heritage centre. Unusually there are two medieval churches within the abbey

Evesham's impressive bell tower and churches

precincts; the apparent reason for this is that one was for pilgrims visiting the abbey and the other was for the local people. Boat trips, pleasant gardens and walks by the Avon – plus plenty of pubs and restaurants – make Evesham a popular riverside resort.

🖋 The walk starts in the market place by the Town Hall and Round House, the latter a fine, timber-framed, 15th-century merchant's house. Walk along High Street and almost opposite the station entrance, turn right **A** along St Mary's Road. Where the road ends, keep ahead along an enclosed path beside the railway line which descends to a track. Turn left on to the track **B**, pass under a railway bridge and continue just above the river.

The track later keeps along the right edge of fields, continues across to Oxstalls Farm and curves first to the right, then to the left and left again, to pass to the right of the farm buildings.

At the start of a concrete section of track by a hedge corner, turn right along the right edge of a field and follow the field edge as it bears left to run parallel to the main road. Turn right over a stile on reaching a tarmac track, cross the road and climb a stile opposite.

Continue along a track – a disused railway – later keeping alongside an orchard on the left. At the corner of the orchard where a track comes in from the left, turn left **C** and follow the track gently uphill for just over ¹⁄₄ mile (400m) to Twyford Country Centre **D**. Among the attractions here are a garden centre, antiques centre, craft centre, falconry and wildlife centre, picnic and play areas and a café.

Retrace your steps downhill, enjoying pleasant views over the Avon valley, to return to the disused railway track **C**. Cross the track, descend steps to the river, turn right and keep along the edge of attractive meadows beside the Avon. After walking beside an arm of the river, turn left through a gap in the trees to rejoin the main riverbank and continue along it, negotiating a mixture of footbridges, gates and stiles, and passing under a road bridge.

On reaching the end of a meadow, keep along a tree-lined riverside path, pass under a railway bridge and soon the bell tower of Evesham Abbey comes

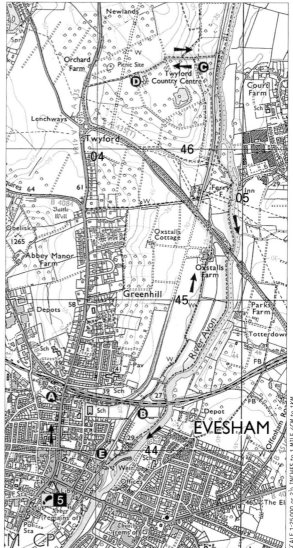

SCALE 1:25 000 or 2½ INCHES to 1 MILE 4CM to 1KM

```
0      200    400    600    800 METRES   1
                                         KILOMETRES
                                         MILES
0      200    400    600 YARDS    ½
```

into view. Eventually the path emerges on to a track – where this bears right, bear left on to a path and go through a kissing-gate to rejoin the river. Divert around a boatyard by a weir, bear right in front of a former mill building to a tarmac track and turn left along it to a road (Mill Street) **E**.

Bear left to a T-junction and turn right up Bridge Street to return to the starting point. ●

Broadway and Buckland

Start	Broadway
Distance	4½ miles (7.2km)
Approximate time	2 hours
Parking	Broadway
Refreshments	Pubs and cafés at Broadway
Ordnance Survey maps	Landranger 150 (Worcester & The Malverns), Explorer OL45 (The Cotswolds)

This short, easy and well-waymarked walk takes you over hills and through woods from the popular village of Broadway to the quiet, immaculate, off-the-beaten-track village of Buckland. It is interesting to compare and contrast the two villages, both attractive and highly enjoyable in their different ways, and there are superb views over the Cotswolds and Vale of Evesham.

Broadway nestles below the escarpment at the foot of steep Fish Hill on the edge of the Vale of Evesham. It is one of the showplace villages of the Cotswolds, despite lacking the attractions of a river, an outstanding building or any well-known amenities. Its popularity lies in its situation and the overall charm of its buildings, mostly handsome 17th- and 18th-century houses. A wide, dignified and long High Street, the Broad Way, slopes down and broadens out into a triangular green around which are grouped houses and cottages, inns, tea-rooms and shops. It was its position as a staging post on the main coach route between London and Worcester that brought prosperity to Broadway in the 18th century; later it became a fashionable place for writers and artists, starting with William Morris, one of the Pre-Raphaelite fraternity and a highly influential artist, craftsman and critic of Victorian industrialism.

🖊 The starting point is at the bottom of the High Street by the war memorial and wide green. Turn along the road signposted to Snowshill and, soon after passing the 19th-century church, turn right along a track **Ⓐ**, at a Cotswold Way sign. Go through a kissing-gate beside a cattle-grid, bear left and head diagonally across a field, crossing a footbridge over a brook and continuing to a stile. Climb it, cross a footbridge, immediately climb another stile, keep along the left edge of a field and climb a stile on to a lane. Turn right and at a Cotswold Way sign turn left **Ⓑ** over the left-hand of two stiles ahead to walk along an enclosed, uphill path.

The path bends first right and then left and continues up to a stile. Climb it, keep ahead along the right edge of a field, follow the field edge to the left and go through a gate into woodland. Follow a path through the wood – Broadway Coppice – climb a stile on the far edge at a junction of paths and keep ahead, still following Cotswold Way signs, along the right edge of the trees. Continue by the field edge to climb a stile, keep ahead to a fence corner, turn left over a stile and then turn right along a track.

Turn right over another stile, keep ahead to climb a double stile and turn left along a straight, fence-lined track. After $^1/_2$ mile (800m), go through a metal gate to a footpath post and turn right **C**, still on the Cotswold Way and in the Shenberrow Hill and Stanton direction. Go through a metal gate, keep ahead along a track and shortly after going through another metal gate, turn right over a stile on to a grassy path **D**. Ahead is a superb view over the Vale of Evesham, with Buckland church nestling in the hollow below.

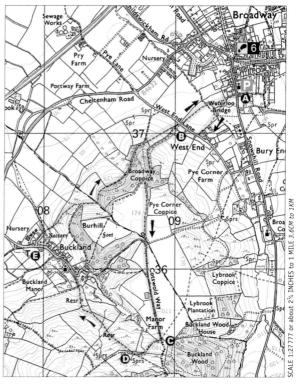

Climb a stile, continue downhill, curving right to climb another stile, and keep ahead, passing through a line of trees, to a footpath post. Follow a series of these posts downhill across the grassy slopes, climb a stile and continue down to another stile. Climb that, walk down a track to a lane and keep ahead through the village of Buckland, passing the medieval church. Next to it is the manor house, now a hotel.

At a public footpath sign, turn right along a tarmac track **E** and where it ends, keep ahead through a gate, cross a brook and continue between fences to a stile. Climb it, keep ahead uphill over two more stiles and continue along a path that contours along the side of the hill, giving more grand views over the Vale of Evesham. The path curves gradually right, following a series of footpath posts and heading steadily uphill to a stile. Climb it, keep ahead and climb another stile into woodland, later continuing along the bottom edge of Broadway Coppice. Re-enter the trees and follow a path to a stile on the far edge of the wood from where there is an impressive view of Broadway, nestling below Fish Hill.

Climb the stile and head downhill, making for the bottom right-hand corner of the field where you climb another stile. Keep ahead down a tarmac track and climb a stile on to a lane, briefly rejoining the outward route **B**. Climb the stile opposite, at a Cotswold Way sign, follow a path across a field towards Broadway church, climb a stile on the far side and cross a footbridge over a brook. Continue across the next field, go through a kissing-gate in the top corner, here rejoining the outward route, and retrace your steps to the start. ●

Upton and the River Severn

Start	Upton upon Severn
Distance	5½ miles (8.9km)
Approximate time	2½ hours
Parking	Upton upon Severn
Refreshments	Pubs and cafés at Upton upon Severn, pub at Newbridge Green
Ordnance Survey maps	Landranger 150 (Worcester & The Malverns), Explorer 190 (Malvern Hills & Bredon Hill)

After a pleasant walk across fields to Newbridge Green and on to the banks of the River Severn, the remainder of the route follows the Severn Way for 2½ miles (4km) along the edge of meadows bordering the river. From many points on the walk there are fine and extensive views across the wide, flat lands of the Vale of Severn to the line of the Malverns and Cotswolds on the horizon.

Dominating the skyline of the pleasant riverside town of Upton upon Severn is the 'Pepperpot', the nickname for the 18th-century copper cupola that caps the medieval church tower, now a heritage centre. The rest of the church was destroyed during a skirmish between the Cromwellian and Royalist forces in 1651 immediately prior to the Battle of Worcester. Although the bridge is modern, Upton has been an important crossing point on the Severn – the only one between Worcester and Tewkesbury – for centuries.

Start on the south side of Upton Bridge and, facing the bridge, turn right through the town centre. Follow the road round a right bend, turn right along New Street and take the first turning on the left, Backfields. Go through a metal gate into a playing field, bear right to head diagonally across it and turn left to keep along its right edge. Continue along a tree-lined track, climb a stile on to a lane and turn right to a road.

Turn right again and at a public footpath sign to Newbridge Green **A**, turn left through a gate beside a lodge and walk along a straight track. After ¼ mile (400m), look out for a stile on the right beside a metal gate. Climb the stile, turn left and keep along the left edge of a field to climb two stiles in quick succession. Continue by the left edge of the next field, go through a metal gate, pass to the left of farm buildings and keep ahead along a track, climbing two stiles, to a T-junction **B**.

The pub at Newbridge Green is to the right; the route continues to the left along a tarmac track. Just before the track curves slightly left, turn right over a stile, at a public footpath sign, and walk along an enclosed path to another stile. Climb the stile, keep ahead along the right edge of a field and about 100 yds (91m) before reaching the corner, turn left and head across the field to a gate in the far right corner. Go through the gate, bear right along a track to a lane, and turn left. After

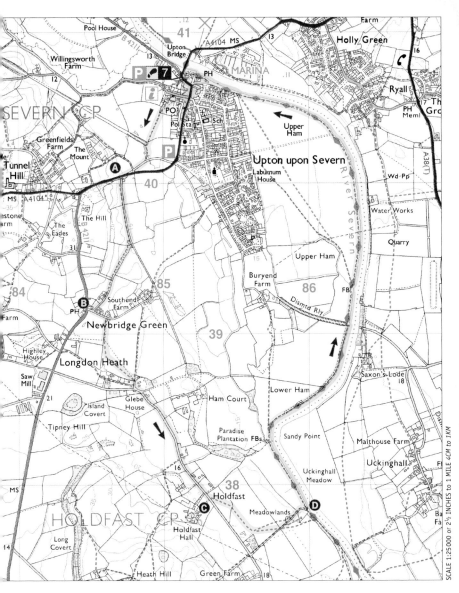

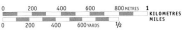

SCALE 1:25000 or 2½ INCHES to 1 MILE 4CM to 1KM

0	200	400	600	800 METRES	1
					KILOMETRES
					MILES
0	200	400	600 YARDS	½	

½ mile (800m), turn left through a
metal gate opposite the drive to
Holdfast Hall **C**. Turn half-right, head
across a field, go through another metal
gate and follow the path ahead across
the next field, curving gradually left to
a stile on the far side. Climb the stile,
turn left along a track, go through a
metal gate and continue to the banks of
the River Severn **D**.

Turn left over a stile, here joining the
Severn Way, and follow it for just over
2½ miles (4km) back to Upton. The
route keeps along the edge of meadows
all the way, following the river around a
long left bend and climbing a series of
stiles. There are fine, wide views on
both sides – to the line of the Cotswolds
on the east and the Malverns on the
west. On the edge of Upton, pass
through a fence gap, keep ahead along a
path, go through a gate on to a lane and
follow it back to the start. ●

Wellesbourne, Hampton Lucy and Charlecote Park

Start	Wellesbourne, near church
Distance	5½ miles (8.9km)
Approximate time	2½ hours
Parking	Roadside parking in Wellesbourne
Refreshments	Pubs at Wellesbourne, pub at Charlecote, pub at Hampton Lucy, café at Charlecote House
Ordnance Survey maps	Landranger 151 (Stratford-upon-Avon), Explorer 205 (Stratford-upon-Avon & Evesham)

On this route all sorts of shorter alternatives are possible. You could just walk to Charlecote and back, omitting the two detours – one into Hampton Lucy and the other through part of Charlecote Park – but the full walk is eminently worthwhile as well as being reasonably short. It enables you to compare and contrast three villages and their churches, and to walk through the deer park in which Shakespeare was allegedly caught poaching. There is also a very attractive finale beside the little River Dene and the chance to visit and explore the National Trust property of Charlecote, with its great house and park.

The walk begins at the top end of Church Street. Go through a metal gate into the churchyard, pass to the left of the medieval church, go through another gate and continue along an enclosed tarmac path.

Just before reaching a footbridge over the River Dene, turn right over a stile and walk across a meadow, veering right to climb another stile. Continue beside the River Dene, go through a kissing-gate, pass under a road bridge, go through another kissing-gate and turn right along a narrow, enclosed path. Climb a stile in front – not the one to the right – and then follow the path as it bends left, keeping parallel to a road on the right, on to which the path then emerges.

Keep along the road for the next ¾ mile (1.2km) and just after a slight right curve, turn left **A**, at a public footpath sign, keeping by a hedge and later a wall along the left edge of a field. Climb a stile on to a road, turn right, passing the entrance to Charlecote Park, continue past Charlecote's Victorian church and take the first turning on the left **B**, signposted to Hampton Lucy. Just after crossing a brook, turn right over a stile, walk along the right edge of a field, climb another stile and turn left along the left edge of the next field.

Follow the field edge to the right, later passing a pool on the left, climb a stile and bear left by a wire fence on the left, heading down through a belt of

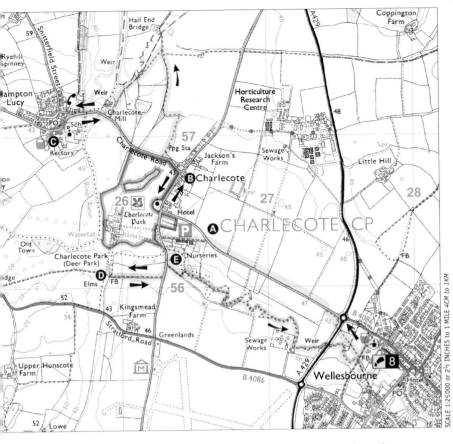

SCALE 1:25 000 or 2½ INCHES to 1 MILE 4CM to 1KM

```
0        200    400    600   800 METRES   1
                                          KILOMETRES
                                          MILES
0        200    400    600 YARDS   ½
```

trees to climb another stile. Turn left across a field, and with the tower of Hampton Lucy church in view, climb two more stiles, bear slightly left, later by a wire fence bordering Charlecote Mill, and go through a gate. Turn right along a lane, cross the River Avon into Hampton Lucy and continue as far as the church **C**. This early and particularly fine example of the Gothic Revival, designed by Thomas Rickman, was built between 1822 and 1826 following the demolition of its medieval predecessor. The apse at the east end was added in 1859.

Retrace your steps to the bridge over the river and continue along the lane back to Charlecote. Turn right at a T-junction **B**, passing Charlecote church and the entrance to the park again, cross the bridge over the River Dene and at a public footpath sign, turn right through a kissing-gate. Keep ahead and at a National Trust sign 'Deer Park Reserve', go through a metal gate and walk across the deer park, by a wire fence on the left, as far as a footbridge over a brook **D**. From here there is a fine view of the house across the park, with Hampton Lucy church in the distance and a glimpse of the River Avon. The mansion of Charlecote Park, home of the Lucy family since 1247, was built in the middle of the 16th century and reconstructed in the Victorian era. The deer park was landscaped by Capability Brown in the 18th century. Although it makes a good story, there is no actual proof that the young William Shakespeare was once caught poaching here.

Retrace your steps to the road, turn left and at a public footpath sign, turn right **E** along a track to a metal gate. Go through the gate, keep ahead and in front of the next gate, where there is a sign 'Riverside Walk', turn left, climb a stile and continue to the tree-lined banks of the little River Dene. Turn right and follow the meanderings of the river around several sharp bends, keeping by a wire fence on the right all the time and at one point crossing a concrete track. Eventually you reach a stile; climb the stile and walk along a hedge-lined path which curves left and then continues across a meadow to a kissing-gate.

Go through, keep ahead under a road bridge, go through another kissing-gate and continue across a meadow, curving left and then turning left to cross a footbridge over the river. Here you pick up the outward route and retrace your steps to the start. ●

The fine Tudor mansion of Charlecote Park

Brailes Hill

Start	Lower Brailes
Distance	5 miles (8km)
Approximate time	2½ hours
Parking	Roadside parking at Lower Brailes
Refreshments	Pub at Lower Brailes
Ordnance Survey maps	Landranger 151 (Stratford-upon-Avon), Explorers 191 (Banbury, Bicester & Chipping Norton) and OL45 (The Cotswolds)

The first part of the route follows field paths beside Sutton Brook and below Brailes Hill between the villages of Brailes and Sutton-under-Brailes. On the return leg you climb gently over the shoulder of Brailes Hill, enjoying fine views across south Warwickshire to the edge of the Cotswolds. There are interesting medieval churches in both villages. Mud can be expected on parts of the walk after a rainy spell.

It comes as a surprise to discover that in the Middle Ages the now quiet village of Brailes, divided into upper and lower parts, was a flourishing centre of the wool trade and the third largest town in Warwickshire after Warwick and Coventry. The main indication of this is the large and impressive 14th-century church, the 'cathedral of the Feldon', which has an unusually long nave and a 120-ft (37m) 15th-century tower.

Start at the war memorial and with your back to the church, turn left along the main road. At a public footpath sign, turn right over a stile **A**, walk along the left edge of a field towards a farmhouse and where the fence and hedge on the left turn left, keep ahead and go through a gate in front of the stone farmhouse.

Turn right along a track, go through a metal gate, turn left and head diagonally across a field, passing an isolated waymarked tree, and continue to the far right-hand corner where you join Sutton Brook. Climb a stile and walk along the right edge of several fields and across part of Brailes golf course, keeping close to or above the brook all the time and negotiating a series of stiles and gates. Eventually bear left about 100 yds (91m) before reaching the far end of the golf course, cutting across a corner of it to a stile.

Climb it, cross a track, climb the stile opposite, turn right along the right edge of a field and climb two more stiles in quick succession. Keep ahead across a field, cross a footbridge over the brook, continue in the same direction and in the field corner climb two stiles in quick succession again. Walk across the next field, climb a stile, keep ahead and climb another one on to a tarmac track in front of a cottage. Turn right to a road in the scattered and widely spaced village of Sutton-under-Brailes **B**.

Turn right, at a T-junction turn left

SCALE 1:25000 or 2½ INCHES to 1 MILE 4CM to 1KM

| 0 | 200 | 400 | 600 | 800 METRES | 1 |
| 0 | 200 | 400 | 600 YARDS | ½ |

KILOMETRES
MILES

beside a large green and follow the lane as it curves right to the medieval church, fortress-like in appearance, with a tower over the south porch. Where the lane bends left **C**, keep ahead over a stile, pass to the left of the church, climb another stile and continue across a field to a stile on the far side. Climb it, bear slightly left

across the next field, climb a stile in the corner and turn right along a track which heads gently uphill. Pass along the right edge of woodland, go through a metal gate, continue uphill along the left edge of a field on to the slopes of Brailes Hill and go through a metal gate in the field corner.

Continue along the right edge of the next field and look out for a blue waymark where you turn right **D** through a metal gate. Walk along the right edge of a field over the shoulder of Brailes Hill, in the corner turn right through a metal gate and turn left to continue along a broad track, passing to the left of a barn. Keep along the track, passing through two more metal gates, and as you continue along the top edge of a field there are superb views to the right, dominated by the imposing tower of Brailes church. Go through another metal gate, walk along a delightful tree-lined path and where it bears right and starts to descend, turn left over a stile.

Head across a field, climb a stile and turn right downhill along the right edge of a field, veering away from it to a stile at the bottom. Climb it, continue along a narrow lane into Upper Brailes and at a T-junction turn right along the main road. You can follow the road back to the start but for a more attractive finale, take the first turning on the left (Castle Hill Lane) **E**.

After ¼ mile (400m), turn right over a waymarked stile **F** and keep ahead across two fields and over two stiles. After the second stile continue along a path, by a wire fence on the left, that descends steps – *it might be slippery when wet* – and crosses a footbridge over a brook. Turn right, head across a field in the direction of Brailes church, go through a gate and turn right along a track to the main road opposite the George Hotel. Turn left to return to the starting point. ●

The view from Brailes Hill

Edge Hill

Start	Radway
Distance	4½ miles (7.2km)
Approximate time	2½ hours
Parking	Radway, by The Green
Refreshments	Pub at Edgehill
Ordnance Survey maps	Landranger 151 (Stratford-upon-Avon), Explorer 206 (Edge Hill & Fenny Compton)

In the fields below the wooded ridge of Edge Hill the first major battle of the Civil War between Charles I and Parliament was fought in October 1642. The walk starts below the ridge and climbs gently and easily up to it. Then follows some lovely woodland walking through the narrow belt of trees that crown the ridge, and on the final descent come fine views ahead, extending across undulating countryside towards the Avon valley.

Radway is a quiet and sleepy village of stone cottages pleasantly situated below Edge Hill, although it would have been anything but quiet in October 1642 when it was one of the closest villages to the site of the battle. Despite its medieval appearance, the church was built in the Victorian era on the site of an earlier one.

Start by facing the green in the village centre, turn left towards the church and where the road bends right, keep ahead along a lane **A**. Through the trees on the left is a fine view of Radway Grange, home of Sanderson Miller, a gentleman and talented 18th-century architect who was one of the pioneers of the Gothic Revival. At a footpath post, bear right along the right edge of a triangular green and keep ahead along a path which passes to the right of a cottage to a stile.

Climb it, walk along the right edge of a field, climb another stile and bear left to pass between

View from the ridge of Edge Hill

a pond and ruined buildings. Continue along the right edge of the next two fields, going through a gate and emerging on to a tarmac track. Cross over, go through a metal gate opposite and at a yellow waymark, bear left and head diagonally across the field to a stile. Climb the stile, continue steadily uphill in the same direction and in the far corner go through a metal gate in front of a house.

Bear right to pass in front of houses, continue along the top edge of a field and where the fence on the left bends left, keep ahead steeply uphill and climb a stile in the top corner. Turn right along a tarmac drive, at a fork turn right over a stile, bear left and pass in front of Westcote Manor. Follow the field edge to the right, turn left through a metal gate, immediately go through another gate and continue along a path – later a track – across an area of young trees just below the wooded ridge.

On reaching the road **B** turn left – *take care as it is a busy road* – and head steeply uphill to the top of the ridge. At a left bend, turn left over a stile **C** and take the path ahead through woodland. For the next 1¹⁄₂ miles (2.4km) you follow a path, well-waymarked with Centenary Way signs, through the delightful woodland that crowns the ridge of Edge Hill, keeping just below the top edge.

Look out for two junctions with tracks: on both occasions you turn left and then bear right to continue through the trees. Finally bear right and head

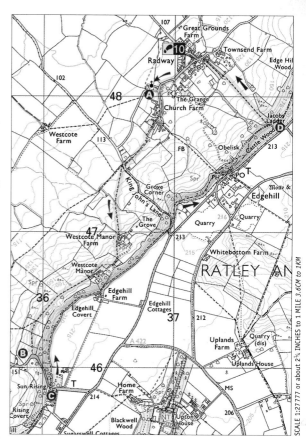

uphill, by a fence on the left, to reach a crossroads to the left of Edge Hill Tower (now the Castle Inn). This battlemented 18th-century structure, built by Sanderson Miller of nearby Radway Grange, overlooks the site of the battle of Edge Hill, generally considered to have been an indecisive encounter.

At the crossroads turn left, head downhill into the trees again and keep ahead as far as another crossroads of tracks **D**. Turn left through a gate and, with a glorious view stretching ahead, walk downhill across a field – later by a wire fence on the right – to a stile. Climb it, keep along the left edge of a field, go through a kissing-gate and continue along a track into Radway. Turn left to return to the start.

Mickleton and the Hidcotes (vertical, left margin)

Mickleton and the Hidcotes

Start	Mickleton
Distance	4½ miles (7.2km)
Approximate time	2½ hours
Parking	Roadside parking at Mickleton
Refreshments	Pubs at Mickleton, café at Hidcote Manor Garden, café at Kiftsgate Court Garden
Ordnance Survey maps	Landranger 151 (Stratford-upon-Avon), Explorers OL45 (The Cotswolds) and 205 (Stratford- upon- Avon & Evesham)

A short but quite hilly walk that gives you the opportunity to visit the colourful and interesting gardens of Hidcote Manor and Kiftsgate Court. From Mickleton the route heads up on to the Cotswold escarpment and continues through the picturesque hamlets of Hidcote Boyce and Hidcote Bartrim. On the return descent there are superb views ahead over the broad expanses of the Vale of Evesham.

Situated at the foot of the Cotswold escarpment, Mickleton has a number of handsome stone houses and cottages and a medieval church with an imposing 14th-century tower and spire. There is a Victorian fountain on the village green where the walk begins.

🖉 Walk along the main road, in the Cheltenham direction, and take the first turning on the left, passing the church. At a footpath post head up an embankment to a kissing-gate, go through and walk along the right edge of a field. Descend to go through a gate, continue through a narrow belt of trees, go through another gate and head uphill along the left edge of a field. Go through a kissing-gate, turn half-right, continue uphill, later keeping by the right edge of woodland, and go through a gate on to a lane **Ⓐ**. Cross over and go up the steps opposite, then climb a stile and turn right along the field edge, which curves to the left. The path bears

slightly right into woodland to continue along its left inside edge. From this point on the Cotswold escarpment, there are fine views through the trees on the right across the Vale of Evesham.

After emerging from the trees, continue along the top edge of a sloping field and in front of a barn turn left to a narrow lane **Ⓑ**. Cross it, keep along the left edge of a field, heading gently downhill, and cross a footbridge in the field corner. In the next field turn left along its left edge, follow it as it twice curves to the right, then turn left over a stile. Walk along the right edge of a narrow field – there is a young plantation here – continue along an enclosed track and go through a gate on to a road **Ⓒ**. Take the lane ahead through the pretty hamlet of Hidcote Boyce and where the lane peters out by a farm, go through a kissing-gate.

Bear left diagonally across a field to a stile, climb it, cross a brook and

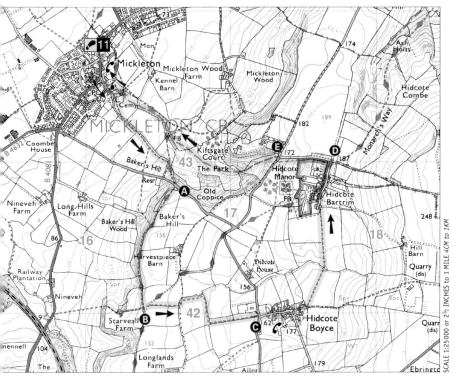

continue across the next field, heading gently uphill to emerge on to a lane. Keep ahead through Hidcote Bartrim, another attractive hamlet with thatched cottages, a duck pond and a wishing well, passing around the back of the manor and garden. Hidcote Manor Garden, given to the National Trust in 1948, is well worth a visit. It comprises a number of small garden 'rooms' separated by walls and hedges, and is famous for its colourful displays and its rare shrubs, trees and roses.

Follow the lane around a left bend **D**, and almost immediately go left through a gate to gain a footpath parallel with the adjacent lane. Keep forward through a small beech woodland to a kissing-gate, and then go ahead, down field, to a gate giving onto a lane not far from the entrance to Kiftsgate

Court Garden **E**, also worth visiting. It was created in the years after World War I and has a dramatic hillside setting with views over the Vale of Evesham.

At the T-junction go through the gate opposite, at a public bridleway sign to Mickleton, and head downhill through a steep-sided valley, making for a gap in the trees ahead where you go through a gate. Continue in the direction of Mickleton church spire, descending to another gate, then go through and keep in the same direction across the field corner to a stile.

Do not climb the stile but go through a gate ahead, walk along the left edge of a field and go through another gate. Keep ahead in the same direction across the next field towards the church and bear left to pass between the churchyard and cemetery walls to a gate. Go through, head down a tarmac track to rejoin the outward route and retrace your steps to the start. ●

Bourton-on-the-Water and the Rissingtons

Start	Bourton-on-the-Water
Distance	5½ miles (8.9km)
Approximate time	3 hours
Parking	Bourton-on-the-Water
Refreshments	Pubs and cafés at Bourton-on-the-Water
Ordnance Survey maps	Landranger 163 (Cheltenham & Cirencester), Explorer OL45 (The Cotswolds)

From Bourton-on-the-Water the route heads eastwards, passing pools which were created by gravel extraction and are now attractive nature reserves, to the village of Little Rissington. Field paths and tracks lead on to Wyck Rissington and the final stretch mostly follows part of the Oxfordshire Way back to Bourton-on-the-Water. There is a striking contrast between the bustle and crowds of Bourton and the quietness and sense of isolation of the Rissingtons.

It is easy to see why Bourton-on-the-Water is such a popular tourist spot. Lovely stone buildings line the wide main street through which flows the River Windrush, bordered by fine trees and lawns and crossed by a number of low bridges. Then there is a bird sanctuary, Cotswold Motor Museum and, behind the Old New Inn, the Model Village – an exact replica of Bourton, one-ninth the size of the original. The parish church of St Lawrence is a mixture of styles – medieval, Georgian and Victorian – and is characterised by an unusual dome on the rebuilt 18th-century west tower.

🖉 The walk starts in the village centre by the war memorial. With your back to the river, turn right and take the first turning on the left, at an Oxfordshire Way sign. Walk along a tarmac track which bears right, enclosed between walls, and curves right again to a road. Turn left and at a public footpath sign, turn right beside a metal barrier on to a path **A**.

At a T-junction in front of the entrance to a cemetery, turn right along a tree- and hedge-lined track, follow it to the left in front of the gate to the Cotswold Carp Farm and about 50 yds (46m) after passing through a metal gate, turn right **B** on to a narrow, enclosed path to Rissington Mill. The path, which passes between some of the pools created from old gravel workings, bends first to the left and then turns right to a gate. Go through, keep ahead across a field, climb a stile and bear right across the next field, joining the little River Dickler and turning left to cross a footbridge over it.

Cross another footbridge, continue beside the wall of the mill on the left, go

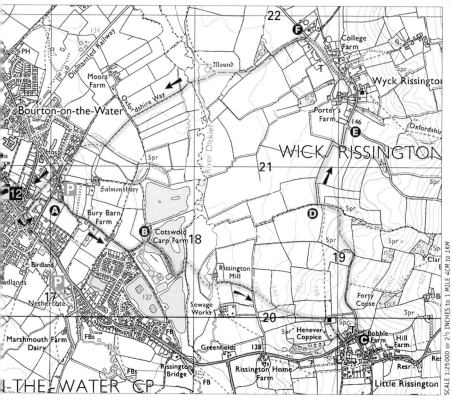

```
0    200   400   600   800 METRES   1
                                     KILOMETRES
                                     MILES
0    200   400   600 YARDS   ½
```

SCALE 1:25 000 or 2½ INCHES to 1 MILE 4CM to 1KM

through a kissing-gate and keep ahead to a stile. Climb it, walk along a gravel track and where it turns right, keep ahead over a stile and continue across a field. On the far side cross a footbridge, bear left, head uphill across a field and climb a stile at the top. Ahead is Little Rissington church.

Walk across the next field, go through a kissing-gate into the churchyard, pass to the right of the small, restored medieval church and go through another gate. Follow the tarmac path ahead into the village.

Turn left along a road and at a right bend, keep ahead along a wide, hedge-lined track **C** which curves left to a metal gate. Go through, bear slightly left across a field, passing a waymarked telegraph post, and head downhill. On the far side turn left along the field edge

and, just before reaching the corner, turn right through a gate and then left along the left edge of the next field. Do not go through the gate ahead but turn right **D** along a wide hedge- and tree-lined track to a metal gate. Go through, keep along the left edge of a field, go through another gate and follow the track around right and left bends to emerge on to a corner of a lane **E**.

Keep ahead through the quiet, spacious and highly attractive village of Wyck Rissington, passing the mainly 13th-century church, the triangular green and the pond, and at an Oxfordshire Way sign to Bourton-on-the-Water turn left through a metal gate **F**. Walk along the left edge of the next three fields, going through a gate and a gap in the hedge, and in the third field bear right, away from the edge of the field, and head across to a gate in the right-hand corner.

Go through two gates with an

intervening footbridge, turn half-left, head across a field to cross a footbridge and keep ahead over another one. Continue across a field, go through a gate, cross another footbridge, go through another gate and keep ahead along the right edge of the next two fields. In the corner of the last field go through a metal kissing-gate to a crossroads, climb the stile opposite and continue along the right edge of a field, turning right over a stile in the corner of the field.

Walk across the next field, crossing a footbridge and then climbing a stile. Keep along the right edge of a field, climb another stile, turn right down steps and turn left along a track to a road. Turn left, at a T-junction turn right and immediately turn left along an enclosed tarmac path. The path crosses a car park and continues to a T-junction. Turn left, at the next T-junction turn right, here rejoining the outward route, and retrace your steps to the start. ●

The River Windrush at Bourton-on-the-Water

The Barringtons and Windrush

Start	Great Barrington
Distance	5½ miles (8.9km)
Approximate time	2½ hours
Parking	Roadside parking at Great Barrington
Refreshments	None
Ordnance Survey maps	Landranger 163 (Cheltenham & Cirencester), Explorer OL45 (The Cotswolds)

A broad, clear track leads northwards over the wolds from Great Barrington, giving fine and extensive views across the Windrush valley. The route then descends into the valley and follows the river into the secluded village of Windrush. From there you continue across fields to Little Barrington, and the final stretch is a gentle climb out of the valley to return to the start. All three villages have interesting medieval churches that retain some Norman features.

To the west of Great Barrington lies Barrington Park, with its great 18th-century house overlooking the Windrush valley. Next to it is the mainly Norman village church which has a fine, 12th-century chancel arch.

📝 The walk begins at the road junction by the war memorial. Facing the T-junction, turn right along the road signposted to Little Rissington and Bourton-on-the-Water and at a public bridleway sign, bear left through a metal gate on to a track **Ⓐ**.

From this broad and undulating track there are grand views over the Windrush valley. After one mile (1.6km), turn left **Ⓑ**, at a waymarked footpath post, along a track that keeps by the right edge of a field, pass through a gap in a line of trees and continue along the right edge of the next field, heading downhill. Pass through another belt of trees, continue across a field and on the far side, turn left along the field edge. In the corner turn right, at a public bridleway sign, and follow a track downhill along the right edge of woodland, enjoying more superb views over the Windrush valley.

At the bottom – just before reaching trees – the track bends left **Ⓒ**, at a blue waymark, and continues across fields. Pass to the left of a farm, turn first right and then left at the end of the farm buildings, and keep ahead. Look out for where a blue waymark directs you to turn right along the left edge of a field. In the field corner, bear slightly left, continue along a track to cross a footbridge over a brook and go through a metal gate. Turn left across a field, bearing right away from the brook and field edge, go through a metal gate and continue across the next field towards

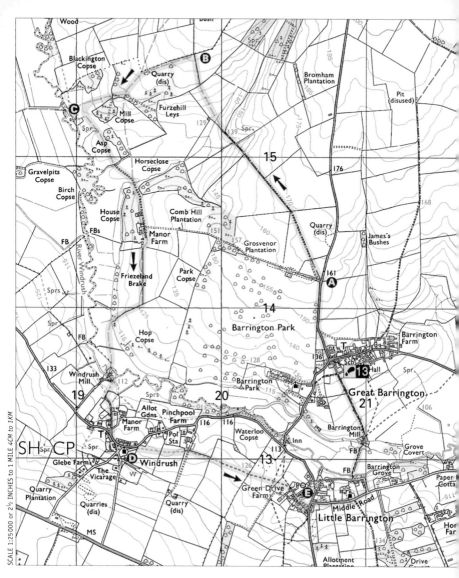

the right edge where you turn right through a metal gate.

Initially keep ahead across the next field and then bear left along a worn path to a gate. Go through, bear left again to climb a stile and keep ahead over the River Windrush to mill buildings. Follow the track first to the right and then to the left, climb a stile, turn right and head uphill along the right edge of a field to climb another.

Keep ahead, by a wall on the left, climb a stone stile and continue along an enclosed path which bears left downhill before heading up into Windrush.

Turn left along a road through the village and at a fork, take the left-hand road, passing to the left of the church. This is a particularly interesting building with a superb Norman south doorway, beautiful 15th-century nave roof and imposing Perpendicular tower which overlooks the small, triangular village green. Where the road starts to curve left, bear right **D** to a kissing-gate, go through and keep ahead across a field, clipping a fence corner. Go through the right-hand of two metal gates ahead, in the next field bear slightly right away from the wall on the left and in the corner, turn left through a metal gate. Immediately turn right through another one, walk along the left edge of a field, by a hedge on the left and after going through a metal gate, keep ahead across several fields and over a series of stiles, finally going through a metal gate between two barns. On this part of the walk Barrington Park is seen over to the left on the other side of the valley.

Continue along a track to a lane and bear right along the lane into Little Barrington. Follow the lane along the right edge of a large, rough, sloping green – once a quarry – to a T-junction, turn left and almost immediately turn right E along a lane signposted 'Church'. Shortly after passing to the right of the Norman church, turn left down a tarmac track which bends to the left. Where it ends, turn right, at a public footpath sign, and cross a footbridge over the River Windrush. Keep ahead through a metal gate and then continue along an enclosed path to cross another footbridge by Barrington Mill.

Pass to the right of the mill and follow an uphill track towards Great Barrington. Go through a gate on to a lane and keep ahead to return to the starting point.

Little Barrington

Otmoor

Start	Islip
Distance	6½ miles (10.5km)
Approximate time	3 hours
Parking	Roadside parking at Islip is possible but you can use the car park of the Swan Inn where food and drink are available
Refreshments	Pubs at Islip
Ordnance Survey maps	Landranger 164 (Oxford), Explorer 180 (Oxford)

Otmoor is a flat, low-lying and formerly marshy area in the middle of Oxfordshire, ringed by seven villages and with low hills on its horizons. The walk explores part of this unusual country that has all the features of fenland terrain: wide expanses, lazily flowing rivers, some of them canalised, and the characteristic straight lines of the tracks and drainage channels. Expect some muddy and overgrown paths in places.

There are few signs nowadays that Islip was once a place of importance. In Saxon times there was a royal palace here, the birthplace in 1004 of Edward the Confessor, founder of Westminster Abbey. Because of this there has always been a close connection between Islip and Westminster: the abbey was endowed by the king with the lands and buildings of the village, and today the Dean and Chapter of Westminster have the right to nominate the rector of Islip.

🖊 Begin at the bottom end of the village by the bridge over the River Ray. Cross the bridge, walk uphill and at an Oxfordshire Way sign to Noke, turn left Ⓐ over a stile on to a concrete track. In front of a gate, bear right along a rough track to a stile, climb it and keep ahead to climb another one. Continue in a straight line across a succession of fields and over a series of stiles, and on entering a large field, bear slightly left and follow a path across it to a stile at a

hedge corner. Climb the stile, head gently downhill first along an enclosed path, then along the left edge of a field, and after climbing another stile,

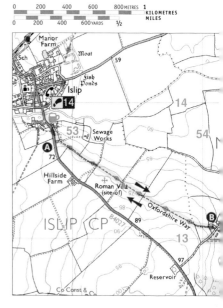

continue downhill along an enclosed path again to emerge on to a lane **B**.

Turn left down into Noke and at a fork in front of the church, take the right-hand lane, passing to the right of the church. Where the lane bends right, keep ahead, at a public bridleway sign, along an enclosed, tree-lined path to a T-junction **C**. Turn left through an area of trees and scrub – this part of the route may be overgrown – to a gate, go through, keep ahead along a track and at a waymarked post, turn right to continue along a hedge-lined track.

Where the track ends, keep ahead along the left edge of two fields, by a hedge on the left, and in the corner of the second field, follow the field edge to the right to keep beside a ditch on the left. Turn left **D** to cross a footbridge, first over the ditch and then over the River Ray, continue along the right edge of a field and go through a metal gate. Cross a track, keep ahead, passing to the left of farm buildings, and the path crosses a tarmac, tree-lined farm drive to a stile. Climb it, continue in the same direction and in the field corner go through a half-hidden kissing-gate on to a lane.

Turn right and follow the lane as it bends left into the village of Oddington, passing to the left of the church. Go round a right-hand bend and, where the lane bends left, keep ahead along a track, at a public bridleway sign to Horton-cum-Studley. Cross a bridge over the New River Ray, a straightened section of the river, and immediately turn right **E** along a straight, broad, hedge-lined track parallel to the river. After crossing a bridge, there is a grand view to the right of Oddington church. Keep ahead and where the main track bends left to a gate, continue along a grassy track to a metal gate. The views across Otmoor are particularly fine. This area was a boggy wasteland until it was enclosed and drained in the 19th century, amidst considerable opposition from the local villagers who lost their common rights as a result.

Go through the gate and continue along the track until you see a bridge over the drainage channel on the right **F**. Cross it, walk along a track towards a farm and pass to the right of the farmhouse to a lane. Turn right into Noke again, follow the lane around a left bend and, at a public footpath sign to Islip, bear left **G** on to a field path. Climb a stile in the corner of the field, head gently uphill along the right edge of the next field and climb another stile on to a lane.

Turn right downhill and at an Oxfordshire Way footpath sign to Islip, turn left along an enclosed path **B**. Here you rejoin the outward route and retrace your steps to the start. ●

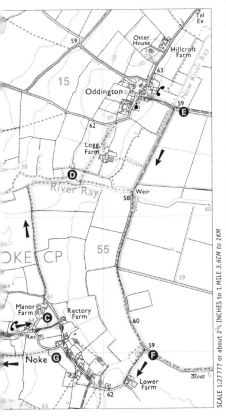

SCALE 1:27777 or about 2¼ INCHES to 1 MILE 3.6CM to 1KM

Alcester and Coughton Court

Start	Alcester
Distance	6 miles (9.7km)
Approximate time	3 hours
Parking	Alcester
Refreshments	Pubs and cafés at Alcester, pub at Coughton, café at Coughton Court
Ordnance Survey maps	Landranger 150 (Worcester & The Malverns), Explorer 205 (Stratford-upon-Avon & Evesham)

The route heads northwards from Alcester through the Arden countryside, via tracks and field paths, to the attractive and historic Coughton Court, a fine country house associated with the Gunpowder Plot. From here you continue mainly across riverside meadows beside the Arrow back to Alcester. Some of the paths may be muddy at times.

Alcester is one of the most appealing small towns in Warwickshire; a varied but harmonious mixture of stone, brick and half-timbered houses dating mainly from the 16th to 18th centuries, with a number of inns and teashops to cater for its visitors. The two most notable buildings in the town centre are the 17th-century Town Hall and the medieval church, with its tall 13th-century tower and surprising 18th-century classical interior.

Start at the top of High Street and walk past the church and Town Hall. Continue along Henley Street, bear right to cross a bridge over the River Arrow and, at a public footpath sign, turn left **A** along a path, between a sports hall on the left and tennis courts on the right.

The path curves left and then bears right to keep along the right edge of two fields – the first one a playing field – and continues along a section of hedge-lined track to enter the next field. Keep along its right edge, following it to the left, and turn right up steps on to a track. Turn left and turn right along the edge of a field, curving right beside the River Arrow and continuing up to a road by an industrial estate **B**. Turn left to cross the river, continue to a traffic island and take the road ahead, signposted to Droitwich.

At a public footpath sign, turn right to climb a stile **C**, walk along the right edge of a field, climb another stile, cross a lane and continue along the gently descending track opposite. Bear slightly right in the field corner and walk along a track beside Adams Pool. At the corner of the pool, turn left along an enclosed path, pass through a gap into a field and turn right along its right edge. Keep along the right edge of the next three fields – going through a gap and a metal gate – and in the corner of the third field, follow the field edge to the

SCALE 1:25000 or 2½ INCHES to 1 MILE 4CM to 1KM

0	200	400	600	800 METRES	1
					KILOMETRES
					MILES
0	200	400	600 YARDS	½	

left, then turn right through a gate. Walk across a field, go through another gate, cross a lane and walk along a track, passing to the left of a house. Pass through a gap to a crossroads of tracks, keep ahead for about 30 yds (27m) and then turn right **D** and head across to climb a stile in the field corner. Turn left along the left edge of a field, go through a gate, keep ahead over a stile and continue across a field. Climb a stile on the far side, turn right along a lane and at a public footpath sign, turn left up steps to a stile. Climb it, walk along an enclosed path, following it around right and left bends, and go through a gate on to a road.

Cross over the road, go through a kissing-gate opposite and continue along a grassy path towards Coughton Court and church. Bear right to cross a track and go through a gate on to a tarmac drive in front of the church **E**. Coughton Court has been continuously occupied by the same family, the Throckmortons, since 1409. They were a Catholic family and in 1605 the wives of several of the Gunpowder Plot conspirators waited here for news of that unsuccessful venture. The most impressive feature of the house is the early 16th-century battlemented gatehouse, beyond which is a half-timbered Elizabethan courtyard with a knot garden. The grounds and gardens are most attractive and the interior of the house has a fine collection of furniture, porcelain and family portraits. The mainly late 15th- and early 16th-century church has a number of Throckmorton tombs.

Turn right along the tarmac drive, passing the 19th-century Catholic church, and go through a gate on to a lane. Go through a metal kissing-gate opposite and turn left to head across the corner of a field, keeping roughly parallel to the field edge. Go through another metal kissing-gate, bear slightly right across the next field, cross a footbridge over the River Arrow and turn right along a lane. Just after a left bend, turn right into the drive to Church Farm **F**, immediately turning right over a stile to head across a field. Go through a waymarked gap and continue beside the meandering River Arrow, following the field edge around left and right bends.

At a right-hand bend in the river, bear left and keep along the right edge of the next three fields, passing through a series of hedge gaps. In the corner of the third field, bear right through another gap, cross a footbridge, continue beside the river in front of a new housing development and turn left to emerge on to a road. Cross over to a public footpath sign **B**, here rejoining the outward route, and retrace your steps to Alcester town centre. ●

Coughton Court

Aston Cantlow and Wilmcote

Start	Aston Cantlow
Distance	6½ miles (10.5km)
Approximate time	3 hours
Parking	Roadside parking at Aston Cantlow
Refreshments	Pub at Aston Cantlow, pubs at Wilmcote
Ordnance Survey maps	Landranger 151 (Stratford-upon-Avon), Explorers 205 (Stratford-upon-Avon & Evesham) and 220 (Birmingham)

There is a strong Shakespearian theme to this walk in the countryside of Arden. It starts by the church at Aston Cantlow in which his parents were married and heads across fields to his mother's childhood home at Wilmcote. Then follows an attractive stretch by the Stratford-upon-Avon Canal before tracks and field paths lead back to the start.

Shakespeare's mother and father were married in the 15th-century church at Aston Cantlow and went to live in Stratford-upon-Avon where William, the third of their ten children, was born in 1564.

Start by the King's Head and turn along Church Lane. Turn left into the churchyard and at a fork, take the left-hand tarmac path to a stile. Climb the stile, walk along an enclosed path, cross a footbridge and keep straight ahead across a field to climb a stile on to a lane **Ⓐ**.

Climb the stile opposite, walk along a track and where it bends right, keep ahead along the right edge of a field and climb a stile on to a lane **Ⓑ**. Turn left and after nearly ½ mile (800m), turn left **Ⓒ**, at a public footpath sign, through a hedge gap to a stile. Climb the stile, keep along the left edge of a field and on joining a track, turn right

along it and go through a metal gate on to a road. Continue along the lane ahead, signposted to Wilmcote, and at a public footpath sign turn right through a metal gate **Ⓓ**.

Follow a track along the right edge of a field and after passing a redundant stile, turn half-left and walk across the field to a waymarked post at the base of a wooded ridge.

Head uphill through trees and bushes, by a wire fence on the left, and just after passing a shed, turn right over a stile. Turn left along a narrow path which bends right and continues (between fences) to a stile. Climb the stile, turn right along a track and at a public footpath sign, turn left through a metal kissing-gate. Keep ahead to go through another one and continue along the left edge of a succession of fields. In the last field corner, keep ahead along an enclosed path to emerge

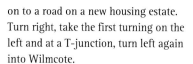

on to a road on a new housing estate.
Turn right, take the first turning on the
left and at a T-junction, turn left again
into Wilmcote.

By the Mary Arden Inn and a small
green, turn right **E**, signposted
Stratford and Henley, passing Mary
Arden's House. This fine Tudor
farmhouse was where Shakespeare's
mother was born and lived as a girl.
Some of the buildings now house a
museum of local farming and rural life.
After crossing a canal bridge, turn left

over a stile **F** and descend to the
towpath of the Stratford-upon-Avon
Canal. This was completed in 1816 to
provide a link between Birmingham and
the River Avon at Stratford. Keep along
the towpath as far as the first bridge,
turn left over it **G**, climb a stile, turn
right along the right edge of a field and
climb another stile.

Keep along the right edge of the next
field and at a waymarked post, turn left
and head across the field to the next
post. Now follow a line of posts across a
large field, heading gently uphill, climb
a stile on the far side and continue
along the left edge of the next field.

Mary Arden's House at Wilmcote

Climb a stile at a crossroads of paths, bear slightly right and walk across the next field to climb another stile. Continue across the next field and near the far corner of the field, climb a stile on to a track.

Turn right to a lane and turn left **H** through the hamlet of Newnham. Take the left-hand lane at a fork and where it ends, keep ahead along a track and go through a metal gate.

Continue along the left edge of a field, pass through a gap and bear left across the corner of the next field to a stile. Climb the stile, keep along the left edge of a field, climb another stile and continue along a track to a road **J**. Turn left – over the brow of the hill the village and church tower of Aston Cantlow lie ahead.

Where the road bends right, keep ahead through a metal gate, climb a stile and walk along the right edge of a field. Pass through a hedge gap, keep along the right edge of the next field, cross a footbridge over a ditch and turn right along a tarmac track to a road **K**. Turn left along the road and follow it back to the start. ●

Barnsley Park and the Coln Valley

Start	Barnsley
Distance	6½ miles (10.5km)
Approximate time	3½ hours
Parking	Roadside parking in Barnsley is difficult but you can use the car park of the village pub where food and drink are available
Refreshments	Pub at Barnsley
Ordnance Survey maps	Landranger 163 (Cheltenham & Cirencester), Explorer OL45 (The Cotswolds)

From Barnsley the route heads across parkland, with views of the great house, and on across fields to descend into the Coln valley at the tiny village of Winson. It continues through the valley to Ablington and then heads over the wolds and back through Barnsley Park to the start. This is in one of the less frequented parts of the Cotswolds, with good walking and some fine and extensive views, but expect some muddy paths in places.

The church at Barnsley is Norman but the tower was largely rebuilt in the 15th century, probably by Sir Edmund Tame, the wealthy wool merchant who, with his father John, was also responsible for Fairford church. Near the church is Barnsley House, the garden of which is frequently open to the public.

Begin at the village pub and take the lane by the war memorial that leads up to the church. Climb a stone squeezer stile into the churchyard, pass to the left of the church, climb a stone stile and bear slightly left across a field to climb another one. Turn left along the left edge of a field and where the wire fence on the left turns to the left, continue across the field to climb a stone stile on to a road **Ⓐ**.

Cross over, go up steps to climb a stone stile opposite and take the path ahead, by a wire fence on the left. Just before reaching the field corner, bear right to go through a gate and turn left along a track. Where the track bends right, keep ahead over a stile and continue along a track which curves right to a metal gate. From this track there is a fine view of the elegant 18th-century house. Go through the metal gate, keep ahead and then turn sharp left **Ⓑ** through a metal kissing-gate. In front of ornamental gates, turn right through a hedge gap and walk along a path, between a wall on the left and hedge on the right, to a stile.

Climb it, continue by a wall on the left, turn left through a metal gate in the field corner and turn right to a fence corner. From here bear slightly right across the parkland, making for a stone stile about 50 yds (46m) to the left of

| 0 | 200 | 400 | 600 | 800 METRES | 1 |
| 0 | 200 | 400 | 600 YARDS | ½ | KILOMETRES MILES |

the field corner. Climb it, descend gently and climb a stone stile in the boundary wall of the park on to a track by a footpath sign **C**.

Keep ahead across a field, climb a stile on the far side and continue across the next field, making for a gap in the wall on the right. Go through the gap, walk along the left edge of a field, go through another gap and keep ahead through trees, curving first right and then left to emerge into the next field. Continue along the field's left edge to a lane **D**, turn left and immediately turn right, at a public footpath sign, through

The River Coln at Ablington

Walk along the right edge of a field, go through another gate and keep ahead to cross a footbridge over the River Coln. Follow a path through woodland, heading up to a gate.

Do not go through the gate but turn right on to a narrow path along the left inside edge of the wood to a gate. Go through that one, bear left and head diagonally uphill across a field, making for the far corner where you go through a metal gate. Continue along an undulating track, pleasantly tree-lined in places, through several gates and later beside the river into the quiet hamlet of Ablington.

Take the first turning on the right **F**, cross a bridge over the River Coln and continue to a T-junction. Keep ahead along an uphill, tree-lined track which levels off and reaches the corner of a lane **G**. Continue along it and at a left bend, keep ahead through a metal gate and follow a track across fields. Where the track curves left on the edge of woodland, keep ahead through a gate and walk along the right inside edge of the wood. Later the track continues through this attractive woodland, then curves right **H** to keep along its left inside edge beside the boundary wall of Barnsley Park.

Go through a metal gate, continue and at a public footpath sign, turn left over a stone stile in the wall, here rejoining the outward route **C**. Retrace your steps across the park to the start. ●

a metal gate. Walk along the left edge of a field, with open and extensive views ahead over the Coln valley.

At a hedge corner on the left, keep ahead downhill across a field and at the bottom follow the field edge to the right and then turn right over a stone stile. Keep ahead over another stile, turn left and walk along the left edge of a field, by a fence on the left, into a dip and up again to a gate. Go through the gate, turn right down a lane and where it bends right, keep ahead, passing to the right of Winson's small and attractive Norman church, and wind down to a small green. Turn right along a very narrow lane which curves to the right, and look out for a public footpath stone where you turn left through a gate **E**.

Bledington, Westcote and Icomb

Start	Bledington
Distance	7 miles (11.3km)
Approximate time	3½ hours
Parking	Beside the large village green at Bledington
Refreshments	Pub at Bledington, pub and café at Nether Westcote
Ordnance Survey maps	Landranger 163 (Cheltenham & Cirencester), Explorer OL45 (The Cotswolds)

This walk, in the gentle terrain of the Evenlode valley near the Gloucestershire–Oxfordshire border, explores some of the quieter, smaller, more tucked-away and less well-known villages of the Cotswolds. There are broad and extensive views over the surrounding countryside and three churches to visit. The walking is easy with few gradients.

The walk starts beside the large village green by the King's Head. Walk along Church Street and where it bends left, turn right **Ⓐ** along a tarmac drive, passing to the left of the 15th-century church. Go through a gate, at an Oxfordshire Way sign, keep ahead to go through a metal gate, walk through a small cemetery and climb a stile at the far end.

Continue to another stile, climb that, keep ahead along the right edge of a field and climb a stile in the corner. Cross a track, climb the stile opposite and continue along the right edge of the next field. Go through a gate, cross a footbridge, turn half-left and walk diagonally across a field, passing through a hedge gap and continuing across the next field to a waymarked post on the far side. Turn right along the field edge and look out for where you turn left **Ⓑ** to cross a footbridge over Westcote Brook. Keep ahead across

a field to a stile on the far side, climb it, continue across the next field and go through a gate.

Continue through a narrow belt of trees and follow a path across an area of rough grass, trees and shrubs. The path bears slightly left, emerges into a field and continues along its left edge, by trees and a brook on the left. Cross a footbridge, keep ahead and climb a stile on to an enclosed track. Turn left along this attractive, tree-lined track, later climbing gently to reach a lane **Ⓒ**.

Turn right, passing the New Inn, and the lane curves left through Nether Westcote up to a T-junction by a small triangular green.

Turn right, follow the lane into neighbouring Church Westcote and at a fork on the edge of the village, take the right-hand lane **Ⓓ**, passing to the right of the restored medieval church. Continue past several farmhouses and cottages to a T-junction, at a public

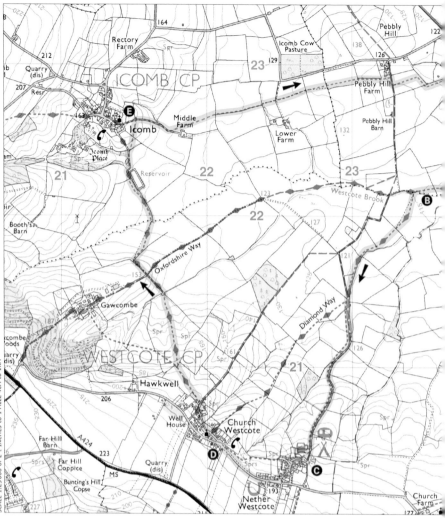

bridleway sign turn right on to a track, which continues as an enclosed path, and after about 20 yds (18m), turn left on to a path through scrub to a waymarked stile.

Climb it, walk across a field, climb a stile on the other side and continue through a belt of trees to climb another stile. From here there are fine, open views across rolling wold country. Keep ahead across a field, climb a stile on the far side, bear right through a tall kissing-gate, climb a stile at a junction of paths and take the right-hand path which heads downhill. At the bottom

climb a stile, go through another tall kissing-gate and continue along an uphill track. Cross a track, keep ahead along the left edge of a field, go through a hedge gap, turn right and head downhill to cross a footbridge over Westcote Brook again. Go through a gate, continue along the right edge of the next field, passing to the left of a reservoir, go through a metal gate and follow a wide track. When the track bears right towards Middle Farm, keep ahead for 30 yds (27m), and then go right, through a gate and obliquely left uphill across a pasture to a gate giving

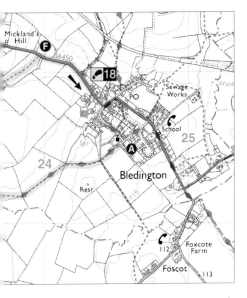

church has a saddleback tower.

The route continues to the right along the track which heads downhill towards Middle Farm, but after 200 yds (180m), branch left at a signpost and through a field gate, and strike across the ensuing arable field to a stile. Keep along the right edge of the next two fields, negotiating a stile and metal gate, and after crossing a tarmac track, continue across the next field to a stile. Climb the stile, keep along the right edge of a field, climb another stile and continue across the next field to climb yet another. Walk along the left edge of a field and climb a stile on to a tarmac drive.

Turn right, at a public footpath sign turn left over a stile, walk across a field and on the far side turn right along the field edge and climb a stile in the corner. Turn left along the left edge of the next field, climb a stile, keep ahead, cross a footbridge and continue across the field to climb a stile near the right-hand corner on to a road **G**. Turn right and then follow the road back to the green at Bledington. ●

onto another broad track **E**. In order to visit the church and village, turn left, then turn right over a metal stile and walk along a grassy path which emerges on to a lane. Icomb is an exquisite little village with a real feeling of remoteness. The restored medieval

The charming village of Icomb

Elmley Castle and the Combertons

Start	Elmley Castle
Distance	7 miles (11.3km)
Approximate time	3½ hours
Parking	Elmley Castle, picnic site and car park
Refreshments	Pubs at Elmley Castle
Ordnance Survey maps	Landranger 150 (Worcester & The Malverns), Explorer 190 (Malvern Hills & Bredon Hill)

Bredon Hill, an outlier of the Cotswolds, is in sight for much of this attractive walk in the flat and fertile country of the Vale of Evesham. The first part keeps along the base of the hill to Great Comberton. You then continue across fields to Little Comberton and on to Bricklehampton, and the last stretch follows part of the Wychavon Way back to Elmley Castle. The route passes through three delightful villages and a hamlet, and there is a chance to visit four medieval churches. In summer some of the field paths are likely to be overgrown and quite difficult.

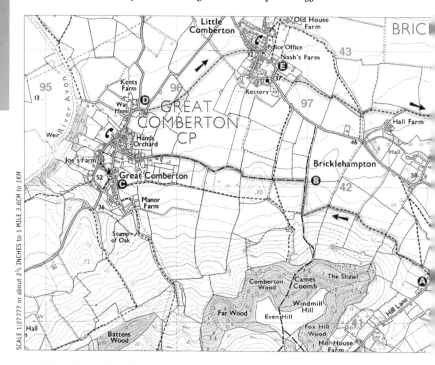

SCALE 1:27777 or about 2¼ INCHES to 1 MILE 3.6CM to 1KM

There is virtually nothing left of the castle of the Despensers from which it gets its name but Elmley Castle is an outstandingly attractive village of black and white cottages, stream and medieval church.

📷 Begin by turning left out of the car park along the lane into the village centre, turn left and almost immediately turn right along a lane beside the Elizabeth Queen of England inn. Where the lane bends left **A**, keep ahead through the gate to Elmbrook Farm, turn right in front of barns, then turn left alongside a barn and go through two metal gates in quick succession. Keep along the right edge of two fields, climbing two stiles, and in the third field turn right over a stile and continue along the right edge of a field to a metal gate. Go through, turn left to walk along the left edge of a field, climb a stile in the field corner and head

straight across the next field. Climb a stile, cross a plank footbridge, bear slightly left, walk along the left edge of a field and in the corner climb two stiles with an intervening plank footbridge.

Keep along the right edge of the next field, climb a stile and turn right along a pleasant, tree-lined track. At a half-hidden public bridleway sign to Great Comberton, turn left **B** along a path – initially enclosed – which later heads gently uphill across a field. From this path there are fine views of Bredon Hill to the left and Little Comberton church to the right, and over the brow of a slight rise the tower of Great Comberton church comes into sight. The path descends gently, bears right along the bottom edge of the field and then curves left to continue along the left edge of a field. Pass through a hedge gap and keep along the right edge of the next field. The path now bears slightly left and widens into a track, which continues along the right edge of fields, later becomes enclosed and emerges on to a lane in Great Comberton, another idyllic village.

Keep ahead to a T-junction, turn left up to the medieval church, walk past it and turn right through a metal kissing-gate into the churchyard **C**. Go through a gate on the far side, continue along an enclosed path to a road and turn right through the village. Turn left at a T-junction, at a war memorial follow the road to the right, keep ahead, in the Little Comberton and Elmley Castle direction, and at a public footpath sign by a left bend **D**, take the path ahead across a field.

Cross a footbridge, turn left and walk across the corner of the next field to cross a plank footbridge. Continue across a field towards Little Comberton, cross another footbridge, keep ahead across the next field and climb a stile in the far right-hand corner. Walk along

Idyllic cottage at Great Comberton

an enclosed path to a road, turn right and take the first turning on the right, passing some more thatched cottages. Follow the lane to the left, passing to the left of the church. This attractive building retains some of its original Norman windows in the nave.

Turn left at a T-junction and at a public footpath sign to Bricklehampton, turn right up steps and go through a kissing-gate **E**. Walk across a field, on the far side go through two gates in quick succession and turn left along the left edge of a field. Follow the field edge to the right, keeping by a hedge on the left, and climb a stile. Turn left, pass through a hedge gap and turn right along the right edge of a field. Follow the field edge to the left and after about 20 yds (18m), look out for a half-hidden stile in the hedge on the right. Climb it, continue along the left edge of a field, by a wire fence on the left, and where the fence turns left, keep straight ahead. On the far side of the field, turn left along the field edge and just before reaching the corner, turn right over a stile. Keep along the left edge of a field, climb another stile, walk across the next field and go through a gate on to a lane in the hamlet of Bricklehampton **F**.

Turn right, turn left through a lychgate into the churchyard and walk along a tree-lined path, passing to the

right of the church. This was mainly rebuilt in 1876 but a fine 12th-century south doorway survives from the Norman church. Keep ahead along an enclosed path into a field and turn right along its right edge. Where the hedge on the right ends, keep straight ahead, picking up and keeping by a hedge on the left, to a tarmac track. From here there is a particularly fine view of Bredon Hill.

Turn left and where the tarmac track ends, continue along a grassy track to a lane. Turn right and at a public footpath sign, turn left through a hedge gap and follow a path across a field, crossing a footbridge over a ditch and keeping ahead towards the trees on the far side. Go through a gap in the trees to cross a footbridge over a brook, climb a stile and bear right across the next field, making for the left edge of farm buildings. Go through a metal gate in the corner, keep ahead to a track and turn right along it **G** to join the Wychavon Way.

Pass to the left of farm buildings and follow the track to a T-junction. Turn right along a lane and where it bends right, turn left **H** along a tarmac drive, at a Wychavon Way sign. Bear left on to a track which enters a field, turn right along its right edge, pass in front of farm buildings and continue along the right edge to a stile. Climb it, head across a field, making for a fence corner, and continue, by a wire fence on the left, to climb a stile in the corner.

Walk along a narrow, enclosed path to a track, turn left through a metal gate and continue to join a tarmac track. Bear right, passing to the right of a pond, and follow the track to the left alongside the Old Mill Inn. Where it turns right, keep ahead along the left edge of a cricket field and pass beside a metal gate on to a lane opposite the car park and picnic area. ●

Bretforton and Honeybourne

Start	Bretforton
Distance	7½ miles (12.1km)
Approximate time	3½ hours
Parking	Bretforton, in the village square
Refreshments	Pubs at Bretforton, pubs at Honeybourne
Ordnance Survey maps	Landranger 150 (Worcester & The Malverns), Explorers 205 (Stratford-upon-Avon & Evesham) and OL45 (The Cotswolds)

Although almost entirely a flat walk amidst the lush pastures of the Vale of Evesham, the western escarpment of the Cotswolds is in sight for much of the way and the views are extensive and unimpeded. The walk uses a mixture of tracks and field paths to link two attractive villages, one with a most interesting old inn now owned by the National Trust. Expect some of these field paths to be muddy after wet weather.

Bretforton is a most appealing and unspoilt village with a wealth of stone and half-timbered cottages. On one side of the village square, called The Cross, is the mainly 13th- to 15th-century church. Opposite is the Fleece Inn, one of the few public houses owned by the National Trust. Originally a medieval farmhouse, it became an inn in 1848 and has remained virtually unaltered.

📷 The walk starts in the village square. With the church on your left, turn left along a lane and take the first turning on the right (School Lane) to a road. Cross over, go through a metal gate, at a public footpath sign, and walk along a fence-lined tarmac path, which later becomes grassy. Pass to the left of a cemetery, continue between fields, bearing first left and then right, cross a footbridge over a brook and keep ahead to a road.

Turn right and, at public footpath and bridleway signs, turn left **A** on to a track that runs along the left edge of a field. After the track turns right, keep ahead, now with a fence on the right, and veer slightly right across the field corner to go through a metal gate **B**. Turn right along the right edge of a field, by Gate Inn Brook on the right, go through a metal gate and continue along the right edge of the next field.

Just before reaching the corner, turn right to cross a footbridge over the brook, turn left over a stile and continue along the left edge of the next field, now with the brook on the left.

Climb a stile, head across the next field away from the brook and go through a gate near the right-hand corner. Walk along the right edge of a field, by a wire fence on the right, to a stile. Climb the stile, keep along a path and go through a gate into the village of Honeybourne **C**.

Honeybourne was originally two villages, each with their own church. This part is Cow Honeybourne and a short detour enables you to visit the

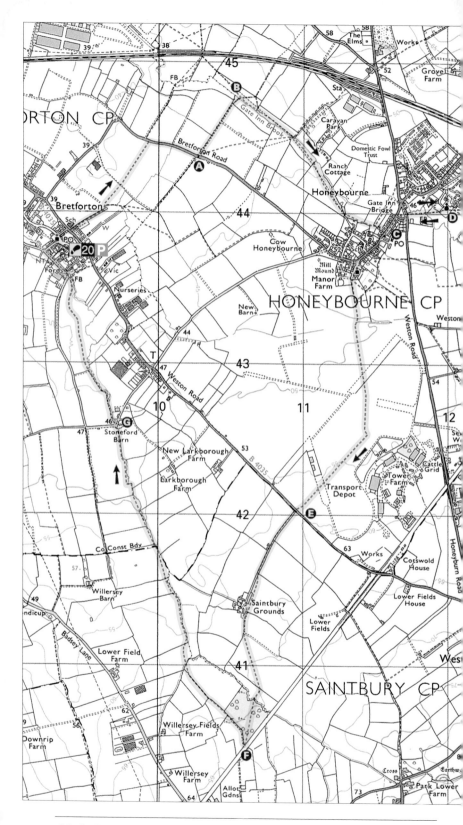

medieval church at Church Honeybourne. Turn left, look out for an enclosed tarmac track on the right and follow this to a road. Go through a gate almost opposite, at a public footpath sign, and take a partly-paved path across a field. In the corner, go through two gates with an intervening footbridge, keep ahead and go through another gate into the churchyard **D**. The church was mainly built in the late 13th century and the tower and spire were added later.

The Fleece Inn at Bretforton

Retrace your steps to where you emerged on to the road in Cow Honeybourne **C**. Keep along it through the village and where it bends right, bear slightly left along a lane beside a green, passing to the right of the church. This was built in the 19th century, although the west tower is medieval, but it is now redundant and has been converted into private houses. Where the lane ends, pass beside a gate, at a public footpath sign, and walk along the right edge of a recreation ground. Cross a footbridge over a ditch, continue across the next field and on the far side, keep ahead across a disused airfield. Some of the old runways can be seen but most of the airfield is now under cultivation.

After crossing a runway to a marker post, turn right and follow a series of marker posts, keeping in a straight line and making for the far left corner of farm buildings. Cross another runway to the left of the farm, keep ahead in the same direction across the final field and climb a stile on to a road **E**. Cross over, take the track ahead to Saintbury Grounds Farm, pass to the left of the farmhouse and, where the track peters out, continue along the right edge of a field, by a ditch on the right. After crossing a footbridge over a tributary ditch, the field edge bears right but veer slightly left and keep in a straight line across the rest of the field, making for a waymarked stile in a hedge.

Climb it, walk across the next field, climb two stiles in quick succession and bear left to head diagonally across a field to a stile in the far corner by the embankment of a disused railway. Climb it, turn sharp right **F** to walk along the right edge of three fields, climbing a stile and crossing a footbridge, and about 50 yds (46m) before the corner of the third field, turn right over another footbridge. Turn left along the left edge of a field, follow the field edge to the right, turn left over a brook into the next field and turn right along its right edge.

Follow the field edge to the left and now keep by the brook along the right edge of a succession of fields – via a mixture of gaps, stiles and footbridges – eventually emerging on to a lane **G**. Cross over the lane and continue along the right edge of fields, still keeping by the brook and climbing over several stiles. In the final long field, head across in the direction of Bretforton church tower – leaving the meandering brook, which you briefly rejoin in the far corner – and climb a stile on to a lane. Keep ahead and take the first turning on the right to return to the village square in Bretforton. ●

0	200	400	600	800 METRES	1
					KILOMETRES
					MILES
0	200	400	600 YARDS	½	

Welcombe Hills and Snitterfield

Start	Welcombe Hills car park, on Ingon Lane about ¼ mile (400m) off the A439, 1½ miles (2.4km) north east of Stratford-upon-Avon
Distance	7 miles (11.3km)
Approximate time	3½ hours
Parking	Welcombe Hills
Refreshments	Pubs at Snitterfield
Ordnance Survey maps	Landranger 151 (Stratford-upon-Avon), Explorer 205 (Stratford-upon-Avon & Evesham)

The gentle slopes of the Welcombe Hills, now a country park, rise to around 365ft (111m) above the Avon valley to the north east of Stratford-upon-Avon and provide a series of fine views across the valley to the line of the Cotswolds on the horizon. After an attractive walk beside and above the River Avon, the route heads over the hills to the village of Snitterfield and continues across them to reach a prominent obelisk, in sight for much of the way and a particularly outstanding viewpoint. From there it is a short stroll back to the start.

An information board at the start informs that Shakespeare is alleged to have invested some of his theatrical earnings in the purchase of a share of the tithes on the Welcombe Hills, and was involved in a dispute over the closure of open common land here.

🖉 Start by turning right out of the car park along Ingon Lane which descends to the A439, turn right along it and then turn left **A** along the track to Cliffe Cottage. Follow the track around left and right bends and at a public footpath sign to Hatton Rock and Hampton Lucy, turn left over a stile and bear right to walk alongside a wire fence on the right. Follow the field edge to the left, climb a stile and continue beside the River Avon.

Pass through a small belt of trees, climb a metal stile and keep along a tree-lined path, beside the river again and below a wooded embankment. This part of the route is most attractive, but take care as the path runs close to the edge of the water. Continue across an area of scrub and rough grass, cross a footbridge over a brook, turn right and head uphill along the right edge of a field. As you continue along the top of a wooded embankment, there are grand views both up and down the Avon and across the valley towards the line of the Cotswolds. Climb a stile, walk through a group of trees and continue along the right edge of a field.

After descending, turn right over a stile, go down steps, cross a footbridge

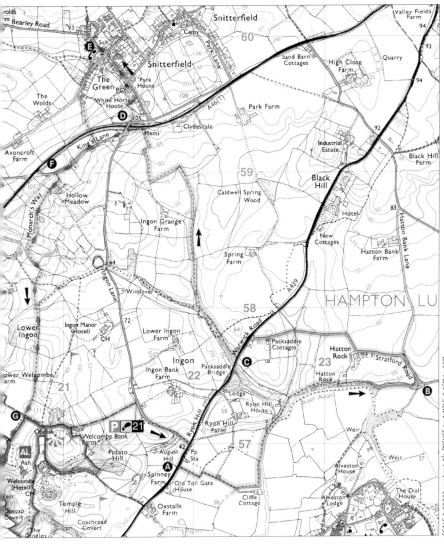

and ascend again to continue along another lovely tree-lined path above the river. The path keeps along the right edge of a field but you need to look out for where it steeply descends the wooded embankment to a track. Turn left along this track, pass beside a metal gate and continue to a lane **B**. Turn left and follow the winding lane for one mile (1.6km) to the A439 again.

Turn left and just before reaching a bridge over a brook, turn right down steps into woodland **C**, descend to the banks of the brook and bear right up steps to a yellow waymark. Continue up and turn left to keep along the left edge of a field above the winding brook. Pass through a hedge gap, keep ahead, turn left over a stile, turn right and head across a long, narrow field, later keeping along its left edge to the corner. Turn left here through a gap, turn right along the right edge of another long and narrow field – now the brook is on the right – pass through a gap and continue along the left edge of yet another long, narrow field. Climb a stile

The River Avon north of Stratford-upon-Avon

orchard, by a hedge on the right, to another kissing-gate. Go through on to a lane, turn right and after ¹/₄ mile (400m), turn left along a tarmac drive to Snitterfield Fruit Farm **F**. Where the drive ends, turn right along a track, between an orchard on the right and farm buildings on the left, and go through a hedge gap. Keep ahead across the orchard along a track which descends and curves left to a fork.

Take the right-hand track, pass through a hedge gap into a field, turn left, follow the field edge to the right, climb a stile and cross a footbridge over a brook. Walk across the field ahead, descend steps to pass through a hedge gap and keep ahead to cross another footbridge over a brook. Continue across a golf course, keeping by a hedge on the left and heading gently up over the Welcombe Hills, and climb a double stile in the top corner.

Keep ahead all the while, over a stile and through a kissing-gate, continue along the right edge of the next field and in the corner turn left **G** along a track. Go through a metal gate to enter the field in which the obelisk, which has been in sight for much of the way, is situated. From here there is a magnificent view looking across the Avon valley to the Cotswolds. The obelisk was erected in 1876 as a memorial to Mark Philips, a Manchester cotton manufacturer who used his vast wealth to build the nearby Welcombe House, now a hotel.

Walk along the left edge of the field, go through another metal gate, pass in front of a farm and the track leads back to the start. ●

in the far corner, cross a footbridge over a ditch, turn left along the left edge of a field and follow it to the right, bending first right and then left and heading up to a kissing-gate.

Go through, keep along the top edge of the next field, go through a kissing-gate and keep ahead to a lane. Turn right to cross a bridge over the A46 and just after a right bend, turn left **D** along a path down to a kissing-gate. Go through, walk across a field, go through another kissing-gate and bear right along an enclosed path to emerge on to a road in Snitterfield. Turn left – the first lane on the right leads to the medieval church, a distance of nearly ¹/₂ mile (800m) – and in the village centre turn left along The Green **E**. In front of the last house on the right, turn left along a tarmac track and, at a public footpath sign, bear right through a metal kissing-gate.

Walk along an enclosed, tree-lined path, go through a kissing-gate, keep along the right edge of an orchard and go through another kissing-gate. Carefully cross the busy A46, climb steps, go through a kissing-gate and continue along the right edge of an

Cold Aston, Notgrove and Turkdean

Start	Cold Aston
Distance	7 miles (11.3km)
Approximate time	3½ hours (shorter version 3¼ hours)
Parking	Roadside parking at Cold Aston
Refreshments	Pub at Cold Aston
Ordnance Survey maps	Landranger 163 (Cheltenham & Cirencester), Explorer OL45 (The Cotswolds)

This walk is in typical wold country, through a landscape of rolling uplands and sweeping valleys, with expansive, open and impressive views all the way. It is an easy walk, mostly on good clear tracks, and all the climbs are gradual. The route passes through three quiet, remote and most attractive villages, all with interesting medieval churches; it can be shortened slightly by omitting the village of Turkdean.

At various times throughout its history, the village of Cold Aston has been known as Aston Blank, but its exposed position, nearly 700ft (213m) up on the wolds, seems to have finally decided the matter in favour of the former. The plain but attractive church mainly dates from the 12th century.

Start at the green in the village centre by the Plough Inn and walk through the village, in the Notgrove and Cheltenham direction. After ½ mile (800m) bear left through a gate **A**, at a public bridleway sign, and walk along an enclosed, straight, tree-lined track. The track is like a dual carriageway, with a line of tall trees down the middle. Pass between gateposts, veer slightly right and continue along another stretch of enclosed, 'dual carriageway' track, eventually going through a gate.

Turn right along a track, turn left

through a gate and ahead is an idyllic view of the village of Notgrove, with the mainly Norman church to the left nestling next to the manor house. Unusually for a Cotswold village church, it has a short spire. Bear slightly right, descend into a dip and head up again, making for a metal gate. Go through and turn right along the left-hand and higher one of two lanes in front, which curves left, passing above the main part of the village and under a lovely avenue of trees, to a T-junction. Turn left and opposite a lodge and ornamental gates, turn right **B** along a broad, gently descending, tarmac track.

After passing a group of barns, continue along a rough track, go through a gate and head downhill to go through another one. Continue, by a wire fence on the right, down to a gate in the bottom corner of a field, go through and now keep ahead uphill

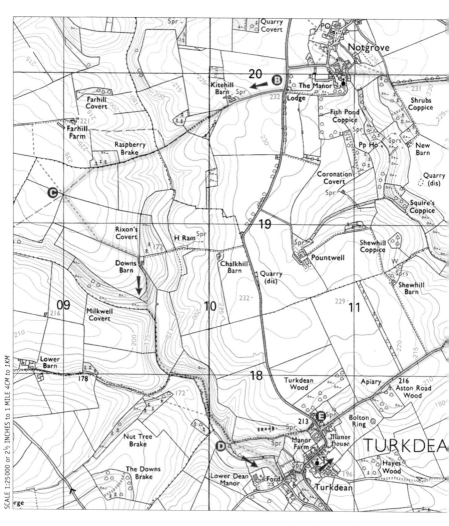

SCALE 1:25 000 or 2½ INCHES to 1 MILE 4CM to 1KM

| 0 | 200 | 400 | 600 | 800 METRES | 1 |
| 0 | 200 | 400 | 600 YARDS | ½ |

KILOMETRES
MILES

along the right edge of a field to another metal gate. Go through that, continue along the right edge of the next field but look out for where a blue waymark directs you to bear left and head across the field to a crossroads of paths on the far side **G**.

Here there is both a stone stile and a metal gate. Climb the stile, bear left to walk diagonally across a field to a waymarked post, bear left again and continue alongside the field edge. In the corner turn right along an enclosed

track, go through a metal gate and continue downhill, cutting across a field corner and bearing left to keep along the field edge to another metal gate. Go through, bear right and follow the curving track through the bottom of a valley, going through a metal gate and later climbing above the valley to reach two metal gates **D**.

*You can continue through the metal gate in front and along the track to emerge on to a lane at the top end of Turkdean, turning right to rejoin the main route at **E**.*

For the main route – which takes you up through the village – go through the

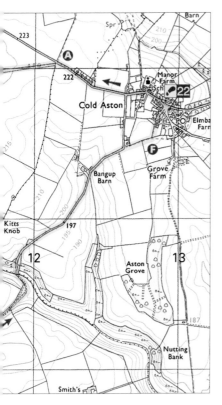

gate in the field corner. Go through the gate, turn left along an enclosed track which, after passing to the left of a house, narrows to a path and heads steeply uphill through trees, curving first right and then left to emerge on to a lane in the small, quiet upland village of Turkdean.

Walk through the village, passing to the left of the Norman church, and at the top end by a small green, turn right along a track **E**, at an 'Unsuitable for Motors' sign.

At a fork take the left-hand tree-lined track and for the next two miles (3.2km) you keep along this undulating and well-surfaced track, crossing a stream and going through several gates. It makes a grand finale to the walk with fine views across the wolds.

Eventually the track becomes a tarmac one and heads uphill. Where it curves left, keep ahead over a stone stile and walk along the left edge of a field towards the houses of Cold Aston. Climb another stone stile, keep along the left edge of the next field and look out for where you turn left over a stile **F**. Walk along an enclosed path, climb a stone stile, keep ahead to a lane and continue along it to the start. ●

gate on the right, head diagonally downhill, go through a gate and cross a footbridge over a stream at the bottom. Continue across the bottom corner of the next field, later keeping by its left edge, with the stream on the left, to a

Rolling wold country near Turkdean

Ilmington and Ebrington

Start	Ilmington
Distance	7 miles (11.3km)
Approximate time	3½ hours
Parking	Ilmington, by the triangular sloping green
Refreshments	Pubs at Ilmington, pub at Ebrington
Ordnance Survey maps	Landranger 151 (Stratford-upon-Avon), Explorers 205 (Stratford-upon-Avon & Evesham) and OL45 (The Cotswolds)

This walk straddles the Warwickshire–Gloucestershire border, linking two attractive villages. It climbs to the highest point in Warwickshire, 856ft (261m) up on Ilmington Down, but all the ascents and descents are easy and gradual. The many outstanding views extend to the Cotswolds, the Avon valley and across south Warwickshire to the long wooded ridge of Edge Hill.

The scattered, warm-looking limestone cottages of Ilmington lie below the gentle slopes of Ilmington Down, the highest point in Warwickshire. The medieval church, mainly dating from the 12th and 13th centuries, is of considerable interest, possessing transepts – unusual for a village church – and retaining much of its original Norman work.

Begin by heading uphill along the top left edge of the sloping green, passing to the left of the war memorial. Continue between houses and cottages and where the lane peters out, keep ahead along a track and turn right over a stile. Bear left, head downhill to climb a stile, cross a footbridge, climb another stile and turn left along the left edge of a field Ⓐ. Climb a stile and continue uphill along the left edge of fields, climbing two more stiles, to reach a crossroads just over the brow of the hill. Ahead is a fine view looking towards the Cotswolds, with the façade of Foxcote House immediately below.

Keep ahead, descending to a stile, climb it and turn right along a tarmac track which curves right to pass in front of the early 18th-century house. The track later becomes rough, winding and gently undulating, and you follow it for 1½ miles (2.4km), around several bends, eventually emerging on to a road Ⓑ. Turn right into Ebrington, an attractive little village with a number of thatched stone cottages and a fine medieval church. Follow the road to the right by the village green and pub and continue uphill.

At the first public footpath sign, turn right Ⓒ over a stone stile, keep ahead to climb another one and, at the fork immediately in front, take the left-hand path. Climb a stile, walk along the right edge of a field, climb another, continue in the same direction along the left edge of the next field and in the field corner negotiate a double stile and double footbridge. Head uphill along the left edge of a field – to the left the tower of Chipping Campden church can be seen

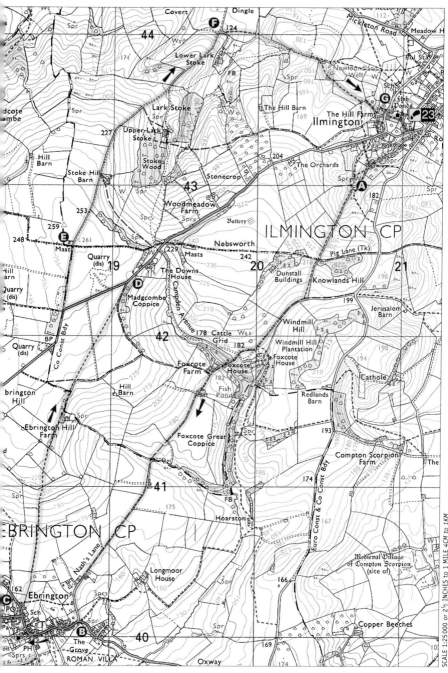

- follow the field edge to the right and turn left through a gate.

Continue uphill across the next field to a stile, climb it, bear right across a field corner and go through a waymarked hedge gap. Keep in the same direction, go through another hedge gap and continue along the right edge of a field, passing along the left edge of woodland sheltering Ebrington Hill Farm. Go through a gap in the field

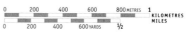

0	200	400	600	800 METRES	1	
						KILOMETRES
						MILES
0	200	400	600 YARDS		½	

Picturesque Ilmington

corner, turn right, follow the field edge to the left and where the hedge on the right turns right, keep ahead across the field. Cross a track, climb a stile, continue across the next field and on the far side bear left along a track, by woodland on the right, to a lane **D**.

Turn sharp left, at a T-junction turn right and then follow a tarmac track up to the radio mast on top of Ilmington Down, a fine viewpoint **E**. Just to the left of the track is the triangulation pillar that marks the highest point in Warwickshire (856ft/261m).

Keep ahead along the tarmac track for the next 1¼ miles (2km), descending gradually all the while and with grand views over the Avon valley ahead and of Edge Hill to the right. At the third public footpath sign on the right – about 200 yds (183m) before reaching a road – turn right along the drive to Upper Larkstoke, joining the Centenary Way **F**.

In front of wooden gates, bear left on to a path which descends, bears left at the bottom and then bears right over two stiles and the intervening footbridge across a brook. Head uphill, veering right to keep along the edge of a valley, by a hedge on the left, and climb a stile. Walk along a fence-lined path, climb a stile, continue along the right edge of a field and after 50 yds (46m), turn right over another stile. Bear left, head diagonally and steeply downhill, passing to the right of a pond, and continue steeply uphill to a stile. Climb it, continue uphill across the next field to a stile, do not climb this one but turn left along a grassy, fence-lined track which bends right to a stile.

Climb it, head downhill along an enclosed track – Ilmington is spread out below – and in front of a farm look out for a waymark which directs you to turn left through a gate. Keep ahead to a waymarked post and continue along an enclosed path which bends right and heads downhill to a road **G**. Turn right, turn left along a tarmac path through the churchyard, by a wall on the right, bear right and the path emerges on to a road opposite the starting point. ●

Warwick and the Grand Union Canal

Start	Warwick, Market Place. Shorter version starts at the Saltisford Canal Trust car park near point **B**
Distance	8½ miles (13.7km) Shorter version 7 miles (11.3km)
Approximate time	4½ hours (3½ hours for shorter walk)
Parking	Warwick. For shorter walk use Saltisford Canal Trust car park
Refreshments	Pubs and cafés at Warwick, pub at Hatton
Ordnance Survey maps	Landranger 151 (Stratford-upon-Avon), Explorer 221 (Coventry & Warwick)

From the centre of Warwick, the route joins the towpath of the Grand Union Canal and follows it for over two miles (3.2km) to Hatton. It continues across fields and later offers fine views of Warwick from the track through the former deer park of Wedgnock Old Park. Although fairly lengthy, this is an easy and almost entirely flat walk. Leave plenty of time to explore Warwick, one of the most attractive and historic towns in England, and its great castle. The shorter alternative starts on the edge of the town.

There can be few finer sights in England than that of Warwick Castle from the bridge over the River Avon, its walls and towers rising sheer above the river. Originally founded by the Normans, the present castle dates mainly from the 14th century, when a major rebuilding programme was carried out. The earls of Warwick were among the most ambitious and powerful barons of late medieval England and one of them, nicknamed 'Warwick the Kingmaker', played a decisive role in the Wars of the Roses. Over the centuries the castle has been extended and modernised several times, especially during the 17th century, and it is now a major tourist attraction. Inside the castle is a fine collection of paintings, furniture and arms and armoury.

Almost as imposing is the collegiate church of St Mary just off the market place. The medieval church was mostly rebuilt after the great fire of 1694 which destroyed much of the town, and is dominated by its magnificent tower. It is fortunate that the 15th-century Beauchamp Chapel survived the fire, as it contains the tombs of several earls of Warwick as well as that of the powerful Robert Dudley, Earl of Leicester, favourite of Elizabeth I. Apart from these two obvious focal points there are plenty of other things to see in Warwick, including the west and east gateways, the outstanding timbered, gabled and terraced Lord Leycester's Hospital, and a wealth of medieval, Tudor, Georgian and later buildings.

The walk begins in the market place by the 17th-century Market Hall, now the Warwickshire Museum. On the west side of the large open area, descend steps, turn left along a road and turn right down Linen Street. At the end of the street, pass through a car park and continue along a track across Lammas Field, now used as Warwick Racecourse and golf centre. Just after passing to the left of the golf centre building, turn right **A** along a grassy path with a line of trees on the left, ducking under several barriers to reach a stile.

Climb the stile, keep along the right edge of a field, follow the field edge to the left and continue along the right edge of fields, alongside a railway line. Turn right over a stile to cross the railway line by a footbridge. Follow a path enclosed between high wire fences, through an industrial estate to emerge onto a road. Keep ahead and to the right is the car park of the Saltisford Canal Trust, beyond which is a visitor centre.

The shorter walk starts here. The canal was built in 1800 as the Warwick and Birmingham Canal, and became part of the Grand Union Canal in 1929 as a result of the amalgamation of several companies. Cross a bridge over an arm of the canal to a T-junction, turn left **B** to cross the main canal and turn sharp right down steps to the towpath. Turn sharp right again to pass under the bridge and keep along the towpath for just over two miles (3.2km). The most striking feature of this part of the walk is the Hatton Locks, a flight of over 20 locks which raises the canal out of the Avon valley.

Leave the canal at bridge 54 – by a car park and a British Waterways yard – and bear slightly right along a track to a

stile. Climb it, head gently uphill across a field, parallel to a hedge on the right, and go through a gate on to a road at Hatton. Turn left, passing the Waterman Inn, and at a public footpath sign turn right **C** along the tarmac drive to Home Farm. Pass to the right of the farm buildings and go through a kissing-gate onto a path above a low slope and then along an enclosed path through trees to

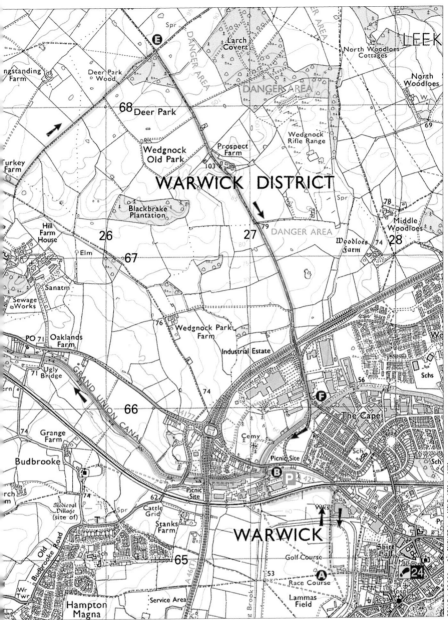

a kissing-gate. Go through and turn right on to a track that keeps along the left edge of woodland. At a junction, turn right to continue by the edge of trees, and then follow the track across a field to meet a lane.

Turn right along the lane, and, at a public bridleway sign, turn left along a track to Turkey Farm **D**. The sprawl of buildings to the right is Hatton Hospital.

Keep to the left of the farmhouse, negotiating some metal gates, continue along a track and carry on to a footpath post. Turn left, walk along the edge of several fields, through a series of gates and hedge gaps, and look out for where you turn left through a fence gap and turn right to continue along the right edge of fields, passing through a metal gate. Finally, after curving left and then right along the edge of woodland and passing to the left of a tree-enclosed pond, go through a gate and keep along the right edge of the next field to reach a tarmac track **Ⓔ**.

Turn right and follow the track for 1½ miles (2.4km) through Wedgnock Old Park, formerly a deer park but now farmland. As the track later gently descends, there are fine views ahead over Warwick, dominated by the tower of St Mary's Church, and to the left the buildings of Leamington Spa can be seen. Eventually the track – now more

of a lane – crosses a bridge over the A46 and descends to a road. Continue along it, turn left into Cape Road and at a canal bridge, turn left down steps to the towpath **Ⓕ**.

Turn right to pass under the bridge, walk along the towpath, then in front of bridge 51 bear right up steps to a road and turn left over the bridge, here rejoining the outward route **Ⓑ**. Turn right into Budbrooke Road to the Saltisford Canal Trust car park and, if on the full walk, retrace your steps to the start. ●

Magnificent Warwick Castle rises above the River Avon

Welford-on-Avon, Barton and Dorsington

Start	Welford-on-Avon
Distance	8 miles (12.9km)
Approximate time	4 hours
Parking	Roadside parking at Welford-on-Avon, by the maypole and triangular green at the south end of the village
Refreshments	Pubs at Welford-on-Avon, pub at Barton
Ordnance Survey maps	Landrangers 150 (Worcester & The Malverns) and 151 (Stratford-upon-Avon), Explorer 205 (Stratford-upon-Avon & Evesham)

Attractive black and white villages, fine riverside walking and wide views across the vale are the main ingredients of this fairly lengthy but easy-paced walk in the Vale of Evesham. The first part follows a delightful stretch of the River Avon between Welford-on-Avon and Barton and then continues across fields to Dorsington. From here tracks and field paths lead back to the start. There are likely to be a few muddy stretches and in summer some of the narrow paths may become overgrown.

A wealth of old, thatched, black and white cottages at its northern end, especially in picturesque Church Street and Boat Lane, makes Welford-on-Avon the archetypal 'Shakespeare Country' village. Completing the idyllic scene is the medieval church, with a fine 15th-century west tower.

🖊 Start at the green and maypole on the south side of Welford, go through a metal kissing-gate almost opposite the green, walk along a tarmac, enclosed path and at a waymarked post, turn right on to another enclosed path. Follow it around several bends, finally turning left to go through a kissing-gate and keeping ahead to a lane. Turn right to Welford church and at a T-junction, turn left along Boat Lane **Ⓐ**.

Where the lane ends, bear left along a path which curves left up steps and bends right to a track. Turn left, then turn right to pass through Mill Field caravan site and climb a stile by a notice 'Stratford to Marlcliff footpath'. The path – narrow and overgrown at times – continues through trees bordering the River Avon on the right and, after the second stile, emerges into more open country. Now follows a most attractive part of the walk as you keep along the edge of meadows beside the placid Avon, climbing a series of stiles and crossing several footbridges. After crossing a footbridge over Noleham Brook, continue to the corner of the meadow and turn left along a grassy track to climb a stile on to a road **Ⓑ**.

Turn right into Barton, follow the road round a left bend in the village centre and where it bends right, keep ahead along a broad track **C**, here joining the Heart of England Way. The track heads gently uphill curving gradually to the left, passes to the left of farm buildings and bends first right and then left. In front of the next farm buildings, turn right on to a path that keeps along the left edge of a field. Turn left, follow the field edge to the right to keep by a hedge on the left and then follow the hedge to the left. Keep along the left edge of fields and, at a footpath post by a hedge gap, turn right to continue along the right edge of a field. Keep ahead to cross a footbridge, turn left over a stile and turn right to continue along the right edge of the next field. Go through a gate to join a track, follow it around left and right bends and continue, between a fence on the left and a line of young trees on the right, to a gate.

Go through, turn right along a lane **D**, which immediately bends left, and follow it around several bends into Dorsington. At a T-junction by the brick-built church, turn left, in the Braggington and Welford direction, and at a public footpath sign turn left over a stile **E**. Bear right across a field, climb a fence in the field corner, bear right along the left edge of a field, by a fence on the left, and cross a footbridge. Keep ahead across the next field, bearing

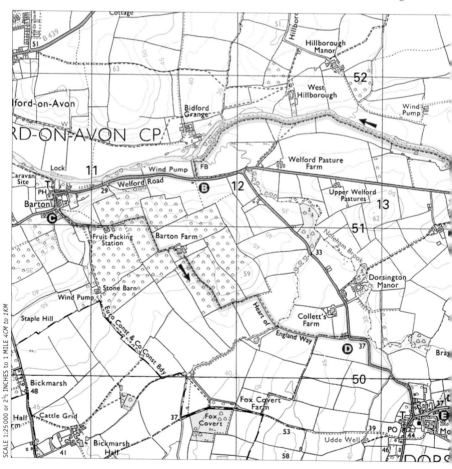

gradually left and making for a stile on the far side.

Climb it, cross a lane, climb the stile almost opposite and walk across a field, making for a stile in the far left-hand corner. Climb two stiles in quick succession, turn right along the right edge of a field, pass through a gap and continue along the right edge of the next two fields, again climbing two stiles in quick succession. In the field corner keep ahead through a gap, go through a metal gate and bear slightly left across the next field, making for the right edge of farm buildings ahead. Go through a metal gate, keep ahead beside a barn to join a track and walk along it, passing to the right of the buildings of Hunt Hall Farm.

Cottages and church at Welford-on-Avon

As you continue along a straight, hedge-lined, tarmac track, the buildings of Welford-on-Avon come into view.

Keep a sharp look out for where a yellow waymark directs you to turn right through a hedge gap, turn left along the left edge of a field and follow the field edge to the right. Just before the hedge on the left bends to the left, turn left through a waymarked gap in that hedge and walk along the right edge of a field to a stile. Climb the stile, keep ahead between bushes and long grass and continue between fences to a road on the edge of Welford **F**.

Cross over, keep ahead along Headland Road and, at a yellow waymark, turn right through a kissing-gate. Walk along a hedge-lined, enclosed path, go through a metal kissing-gate and keep ahead to return to the start. ●

Hay Wood, Rowington and Baddesley Clinton

Start	Forestry Commission's Hay Wood car park, off Hay Wood Lane 1 mile (1.6km) south of Baddesley Clinton village
Distance	8 miles (12.9km). Two shorter versions of 3½ miles (5.6km) and 5 miles (8km)
Approximate time	4 hours (1½ hours and 2½ hours for shorter walks)
Parking	Hay Wood
Refreshments	Pub by first canal bridge, pub where the route leaves the canal near point **G**, café at Baddesley Clinton Hall
Ordnance Survey maps	Landranger 139 (Birmingham & Wolverhampton), Explorers 220 (Birmingham) and 221 (Coventry & Warwick)

A walk through Hay Wood leads to the parkland of Wroxall Abbey with its Victorian house, medieval church and scanty monastic remains. The route continues across fields to the hilltop church at Rowington and then follows an attractive stretch of the Grand Union Canal. The final part of the walk brings you to Baddesley Clinton where there is an opportunity to visit a picturesque moated manor house. This walk, in the countryside of the old Forest of Arden, can be split into two separate shorter walks if desired.

*For the 5-mile (8km) alternative walk, turn left from the car park along the lane and take the first lane on the right to join the main route at **D**.*

For the 3½ mile (5.6km) walk and the full walk, turn right out of the car park along the lane and just after passing the turning on the left to Baddesley Clinton church, turn right **A**, at a public footpath sign, on to a track that leads into Hay Wood. Go through a gate by a cottage, walk along a path that later broadens into a track and, at a crossroads, keep ahead along the

bridleway through this attractive area of mixed woodland.

Bear right to emerge from the wood via a gate, veer left and head across a field to another gate. Go through, continue along a track to a T-junction and turn left along a tarmac drive. Bear right in front of a half-timbered farmhouse, go through a gate and continue along the tarmac drive to a road **B**. Turn right and after ½ mile (800m), turn right again on to a track. Climb a stile, go through a gate and continue along the track as far as a

Baddesley Clinton: moat, bridge and gatehouse

waymarked post **C**.

At this point turn left for a brief detour to Wroxall church and abbey ruins. Walk across the grass, keeping parallel to an avenue of trees on the right, go through a kissing-gate, continue along a tarmac drive, by a wall on the right, and at a crossroads turn right. The red brick Victorian mansion of Wroxall Abbey – now a conference and leisure centre – is ahead, and on either side of the drive are the church and fragments of the 12th-century Benedictine nunnery. The church is the north aisle of the former abbey – the brick west tower was added in the 17th century.

Retrace your steps to the waymarked post **C**, turn left and continue along the track, bearing right to a kissing-gate. Go through, keep ahead across a field, go through another kissing-gate, walk through a circle of trees and go through a kissing-gate on the far side. Head across the parkland to the next waymarked post and continue downhill to a stile on the left edge of a belt of trees. Climb it, walk across a field, climb

SCALE 1:25000 or 2½ INCHES to 1 MILE 4CM to 1KM

another stile, keep along the right edge
of a field and go through a metal gate
on to a lane. Turn right and take the
first turning on the left, signposted
Rowington and Lapworth **D**.

*Keep ahead here to return to the start
if following the 3¹/₂-mile (5.5km)
alternative. Join the full walk here if
doing the 5-mile (8km) alternative.*

At a Heart of England Way sign, turn
left through a metal gate, walk across a
field to a stile on the far side, climb it
and continue in the same direction
across the next field, heading gently
downhill and making for a waymarked
post in a fence. Turn left alongside the
fence and at a corner follow the field

edge to the right and continue down to
a metal gate.

Go through, head uphill across a
field, climb a stile and continue across
the next field, keeping just to the right
of a line of fine old trees. Rowington
church tower is ahead. At a fence
corner, keep by a wire fence and hedge
on the left to descend to a stile. Climb it,
head gently uphill along the left edge of
a field, turn left over a stile in the
corner and continue along the top edge
of a field to climb a stile into
Rowington churchyard. Walk through
it, bearing right to pass to the right of
the handsome, mainly 13th-century,
cruciform church.

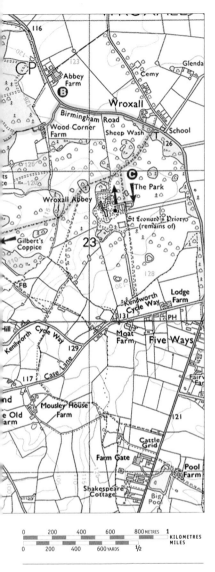

and Stratford-upon-Avon canals, then at bridge 65 bear left up steps on to a road and turn right over the bridge **G**.

At a public footpath sign turn left over a stile, walk along a track, climb another stile and continue along the track to where you bear right, in front of a brick building, to a stile. Climb it, head diagonally across a large field, climb a stile in the far corner, continue along the right edge of a field and climb two stiles in quick succession. Keep ahead over another stile and as you continue along the right edge of a field, Baddesley Clinton can be seen through the trees on the right. Where the fence turns right, veer slightly right, head across a field and climb a stile in the far corner on to a drive **H**.

Turn sharp right to walk along the left-hand of the two drives ahead to the entrance to the house. Baddesley Clinton, surrounded by a moat and with a bridge leading to a battlemented gatehouse, looks the perfect medieval manor house. The oldest part dates back to the 14th century, and it has changed little since the middle of the 17th century. During its long history it has mainly been ocupied by two families, the Bromes and Ferrers, and inside are portraits of the families, plus priest holes and a chapel.

In front of the entrance turn left, at 'To the Church' and Heart of England Way signs, along an attractive, tree-lined path. Go through a gate into the churchyard and follow a tarmac path to the right of the mainly 15th-century church, built by Nicolas Brome as a penance for the murder of a local priest in 1485. It contains graves and memorials to members of the Bromes and Ferrers families.

Turn right to go through another gate and continue first along a tarmac path, then along a tree-lined drive, to a lane. Turn right again to return to the start. ●

On emerging on to a road turn left **E** and where the road soon bends left, continue ahead along a tarmac track that descends to a stile. Climb it and keep ahead to cross a canal bridge **F**. Turn left over a stile to descend to the towpath, turn sharp left, pass under the bridge and walk along the towpath of the Grand Union Canal for the next 1¾ miles (2.8km). The canal flows initially between steep wooded banks and later crosses flatter, more open country. Cross a footbridge over a short side canal that links the Grand Union

Stratford-upon-Avon and the Stour Valley

Start	Stratford-upon-Avon (Clifford Chambers for one of the two shorter alternatives)
Distance	9 miles (14.5km). Can be split into two separate walks of 4½ miles (7.2km) each
Approximate time	4½ hours (2¼ hours for each of the shorter walks)
Parking	Stratford-upon-Avon, or roadside parking in Clifford Chambers
Refreshments	Pubs and cafés at Stratford-upon-Avon, restaurant at the Shire Horse Centre, pub at Clifford Chambers
Ordnance Survey maps	Landranger 151 (Stratford-upon-Avon), Explorer 205 (Stratford-upon-Avon & Evesham)

This walk in the heart of Shakespeare Country explores the attractive Stour valley to the south of Stratford-upon-Avon. It begins by following the track of a disused tramway and field paths, first to the Shire Horse Centre and then on to the village of Clifford Chambers. From there the route does a circuit, passing through two quiet villages, before returning to Clifford Chambers, and then heads down into the Avon valley for a lovely and relaxing finale by the river. As this is a figure-of-eight route, it can be split into two shorter separate walks, one returning directly to Stratford from Clifford Chambers, and the other starting from Clifford Chambers and omitting Stratford.

Even if Shakespeare had not been born here, Stratford's wealth of half-timbered Tudor buildings and picturesque riverside location would still make it a major tourist attraction. But you can never escape the fact that he was born here: Shakespeare's influence permeates the whole town and has made it one of the world's great centres of literary pilgrimage. Throughout Stratford are various buildings and monuments that illustrate almost all the stages in Shakespeare's life, and more especially the huge industry that has grown up in the centuries following his death. There

is his father's prosperous 16th-century house, where Shakespeare was born in 1564; the Grammar School and adjoining 15th-century Guild Chapel, where he went to school; the 15th-century Clopton Bridge he crossed on his way to London; the foundations and gardens of New Place, where he lived during the latter part of his life and where he died; the splendid half-timbered Hall's Croft, where his daughter Susanna and her husband lived; and the medieval Holy Trinity Church, by the river, in which he is buried. More recent are the 19th-century statue of him in the riverside gardens and the Royal Shakespeare Theatre, rebuilt in 1932 after fire destroyed its Victorian predecessor.

👞 The walk starts at Shakespeare's statue. Facing the road, turn right, after a few yards bear right along a tarmac track and cross the brick Tramway Bridge over the River Avon. Keep ahead to cross a road, and for just over ½ mile (800m) you walk along a straight, tree-lined tarmac track on top of an embankment, later running parallel to a road on the left. This track was part of the Stratford and Moreton Tramway, a horse-drawn tramway built in the early 19th century.

Eventually the track emerges on to the road at a junction. Cross over the road, keep ahead along a hedge-lined path to emerge on to the road again at another junction and turn right along the B4632, signposted to Broadway and Mickleton.

Holy Trinity Church, Stratford-upon-Avon

After 200 yds (183m), turn left over a stile **Ⓐ** and bear slightly right across the corner of a field. Turn right on the far side, follow the field edge to the right again and then bear left, still along the field edge. Follow the track through a hedge gap into the next field and continue across it to the Shire Horse Centre and Farm Park **Ⓑ**. Here you can watch the shire horses at work and there are also pony rides and rare breeds of farm animals.

In front of the centre turn left along a track, pass between barns and, at the end of the last barn, turn right on to another track, heading towards Clifford Chambers. Climb a stile and turn left along the left edge of a field, bearing right away from it and descending towards the river. Climb a stile, keep ahead, climb another and continue across the next field, turning right to cross a footbridge over the River Stour. Go through a metal gate, turn right along an enclosed path above the river and turn left along a track. Go through a kissing-gate, pass in front of a house across the end of a pool and the path bends right to a gate. Go through, continue along a track to the bottom end of the main street in Clifford Chambers and turn right. Clifford Chambers is a most attractive village with a medieval church and a long, wide street, bordered by a green and lined with timber-framed cottages.

One of the shorter alternatives keeps ahead here, following route directions from point **Ⓖ**. *The other alternative starts from here and follows directions from point* **Ⓒ**.

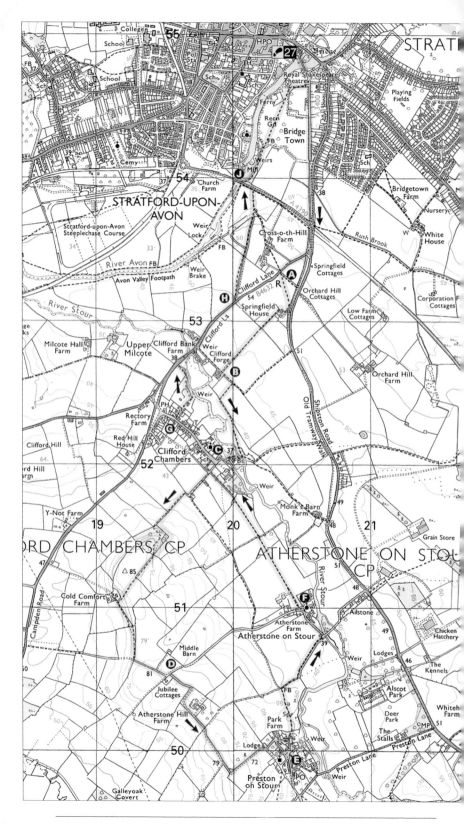

Take the first turning on the left **C** and walk along a grassy, hedge-lined track. At a T-junction turn left, climb a stile, turn right on to a track and take the right-hand path at a fork. The path turns left, then heads gently uphill along the right edge of a field, and in the top corner follow the field edge first to the left and then to the right. At the next corner keep ahead through a gap, continue along the left edge of a field, pass through a hedge gap on the left and keep in the same direction along the right edge of a field. From here there is a very good view ahead over the Avon valley.

Descend to the field corner, follow the field edge to the left, bear left through a hedge gap in the next corner, turn right and walk across a field, making for a stile just to the right of a conifer plantation. Climb it, turn left along a track, climb another stile, turn left at a T-junction, then a few yards ahead turn right along a narrow lane **D**. Follow it for ³/₄ mile (1.2km) – there are several sharp bends – into Preston on Stour; the final right bend brings you to the village green and church. The medieval church has a Perpendicular tower but was partially rebuilt in the 18th century.

At a T-junction by the green turn sharp left **E** and where the lane ends, keep ahead along a path to a kissing-gate. Go through the gate and as you walk across a field there is a fine view to the right across the Stour valley to Alscot Park, an early example of the Gothic revival. Go through a gate, continue along the right edge of a field and in the field corner turn right on to a winding, enclosed path that emerges on to a lane in front of a bridge over the River Stour.

Turn left into Atherstone on Stour and just after the lane bends left by the small Victorian church, turn right **F** along a straight track. Go through a hedge gap into a field and walk across it, passing to the right of a solitary tree and making for a brick building on the far side. Go through a gate, continue along an enclosed path to a track, cross it and climb a stile, here briefly rejoining the outward route. Keep ahead along a path and turn right on to a grassy track back into Clifford Chambers **C**.

Turn left along the village street, passing the church, and about 100 yds (91m) before the pub, turn right **G**, at a public footpath sign, along a tarmac drive. Where this ends, keep ahead across grass, descending to the River Stour again, and at a public footpath sign, turn left along the bottom edge of a field to a gate. Go through, continue above the river, passing through two kissing-gates, and keep along the right edge of a field to climb a stile on to a road. Turn right, cross the Stour and after nearly ¹/₂ mile (800m), turn left over a stile **H**. Walk across a narrow field and on the other side turn right along its left edge, parallel to a track on the other side of the boundary fence.

Go through a gate and, with a fine view ahead over Stratford and the Avon valley, head downhill along a fence-lined tarmac path to a stile. Climb it, turn left to continue below a road embankment and, on reaching the Avon, turn right on to a riverside path **J**, passing under a road bridge.

Now comes a most attractive finale as you follow a delightful path beside the river along the edge of a recreation area, passing – on the opposite bank – Holy Trinity Church and later the Royal Shakespeare Theatre. Finally turn left over the Tramway Bridge to return to the Shakespeare statue. ●

0   200   400   600   800 METRES 1
████████████████████████████████ KILOMETRES
                                  MILES
0   200   400   600 YARDS   ¹/₂

Burton Dassett Hills and the surrounding villages

Burton Dassett Hills and the surrounding villages

Start	Burton Dassett Hills Country Park
Distance	8½ miles (13.7km)
Approximate time	4½ hours
Parking	Burton Dassett Hills Country Park
Refreshments	Pub at Fenny Compton, pub at Farnborough, pub at Avon Dassett
Ordnance Survey maps	Landranger 151 (Stratford-upon-Avon), Explorer 206 (Edge Hill & Fenny Compton)

Three beautiful limestone villages, four medieval churches, the chance to visit an 18th-century hall and superb views over the Warwickshire countryside all add up to a highly scenic, varied and enjoyable walk. From the open slopes of the Burton Dassett Hills, the route descends into Fenny Compton and continues, via a mixture of field paths, tracks and quiet lanes, to Farnborough, with its great house. The rest of the walk mainly contours along the side of hills to Avon Dassett and on to return to the start, passing the isolated and atmospheric church at Burton Dassett.

The smooth, rounded slopes of the Burton Dassett Hills provide a series of extensive views over the surrounding Midlands countryside, and both Warwick Castle and Coventry Cathedral can be seen from here. Some of the hollows visible are the remains of abandoned quarries.

[✎] The walk begins by the 16th-century Beacon Tower on Windmill Hill, and it is certainly worthwhile climbing the steps for the magnificent view that the extra height brings.

Descend the steps, turn right along the lane and at a fork, take the left-hand lane, signposted Avon Bassett, Fenny Compton and Farnborough, heading gently uphill. About 200 yds (183m) after passing a barn on the left, turn left **Ⓐ** through a metal gate and

head diagonally and steeply downhill in the direction of the right edge of the trees ahead. Skirt a fence corner, continue down to go through a metal gate and follow a path through an attractive valley, with the woodland of Burton Old Covert on the left, curving left to reach a hedge.

Turn right alongside the hedge, go through a metal gate and continue gently downhill along the left edge of a field towards Fenny Compton. Go through a metal gate in the bottom corner, walk across the next field, go through another metal gate by a barn and keep ahead along a track which bends right to a road in Fenny Compton, a most attractive village of warm looking stone cottages. The medieval church has a 14th-century tower crowned by a short spire.

Turn right, take the first turning on the left (Church Street), turn right along Dog Lane **B**, passing to the right of the church, and go through a gate at a public footpath sign. Walk along the top edge of a field, by the churchyard wall and later an iron fence on the left, and at the corner of this fence bear left and head across to a stile.

Isolated Burton Dassett church

Climb the stile, walk across a field to climb another one and continue uphill in the same direction across the next field, making for the left corner of the garden hedge in front. Bear left across the field corner to a stile, climb it, cross a concrete track, go through a metal gate opposite and walk across a field to a stile. Climb the stile, keep along the left edge of a field, by a fence on the left, and where the fence turns left continue in the same direction – cutting across the field corner – to climb a stile. Bear left along the left edge of the next field and in the corner keep ahead along an enclosed path which bears right through trees to a stile. Climb it and turn left along a track, passing to the right of a pond. Where the track bends left, keep ahead to continue along the left edge of the next field.

At the bottom end of the field, turn left along a track and at a hedge gap on the right, bear right and head diagonally across a field to go through another hedge gap on the far side. Continue across the corner of the next field, passing to the right of a pond, to emerge on to a road **C** and take the lane ahead, signposted Claydon.

After ¾ mile (1.2km) – where the lane curves left – turn right through a metal gate **D**, at a public bridleway sign, bear slightly right and walk across a field to a metal gate. Go through the gate, keep

in the same direction across the next field, veering left to cross a ditch, and go through a metal gate in the corner.

Continue across the next long field, heading towards the hedge on the left side, go through another metal gate in the corner of the field, continue across a field, go through a metal gate and keep along the right edge of the next field, joining a track and following it up to a road **E**.

Keep ahead along the lane opposite into Farnborough, going round several bends and passing to the right of the attractive, medieval church. At a fork take the right-hand lane down to a T-junction **F** – ahead is a grand view of Farnborough Hall, an elegant 18th-century house belonging to the National Trust. The grounds are particularly fine, containing several Classical temples.

Turn right, follow the lane to the left across part of the park, passing between lakes and woodland, and after roughly ½ mile (800m), turn right through a metal gate **G**, at a public footpath sign. Bear left and head diagonally uphill across a field towards the right corner

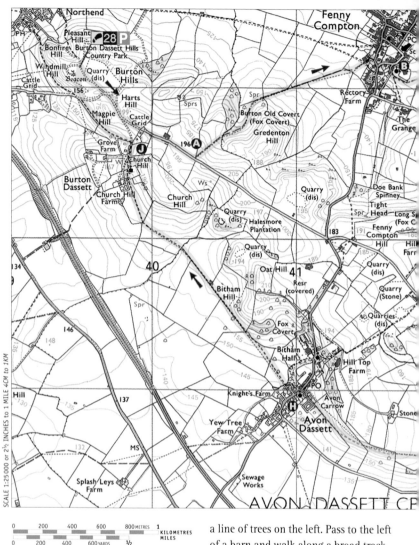

SCALE 1:25 000 or 2½ INCHES to 1 MILE 4CM to 1KM

0 200 400 600 800 METRES 1 KILOMETRES
0 200 400 600 YARDS ½ MILES

of a group of trees. Climb a stile at the top, keep ahead across the next field and climb a stile by a hedge corner. As you continue along the top edge of a field, there are grand views to the left across to the ridge of Edge Hill.

At the far end of the field turn left over a stile, turn right and continue across the grassy slopes, veering away from the top right edge and making for the lower left edge, continuing past a waymark to a stile. Climb the stile, walk along the left edge of a field, go through a metal gate and keep ahead by

a line of trees on the left. Pass to the left of a barn and walk along a broad track to reach a lane in Avon Dassett. The parish church, mostly rebuilt in the Victorian period, is to the right; the route continues to the left down to the Prince of Wales pub.

By the pub turn right along Park Close ⒽMETR and where the lane ends, go through a metal gate and keep ahead across a field to a stile. Climb the stile, continue across the next field towards the wooded Bitham Hill, on the far side bear left and continue along the field edge to a stile. Climb the stile and keep along the right edge of the next two fields, climbing another stile, and in the

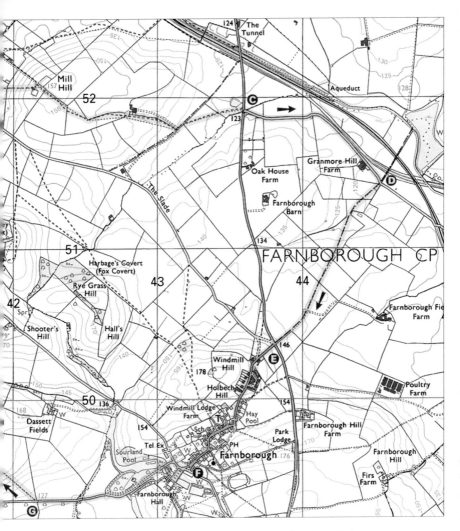

corner of the second field descend to cross a footbridge. Continue across the next field, curving left to keep below the slopes on the right, and climb another stile. Burton Dassett church can be seen ahead.

Walk across a field towards the church, climb a stile in a fence on the right and continue in the same direction across a succession of fields and over a series of stiles, finally climbing a stone stile into the churchyard. The plain, isolated church, mainly built in the late 12th and 13th centuries, is exceptionally unspoilt and retains two of its original Norman doorways. In the Middle Ages it was at the centre of a

prosperous village but this became depopulated, partly because of the Black Death but mainly through the forcible evictions carried out in the 16th century by Sir Edward Belknap, who wanted the land for more lucrative sheep farming.

Pass in front of the church, go through a kissing-gate and walk along a track to a lane. Keep along it as far as a cattle-grid **J**, turn left along the left edge of a field and where the wire fence on the left turns left, continue ahead, later rejoining the fence and keeping alongside it to a lane. From here make your way across the smooth grassy slopes in front to the start. ●

Further Information

The National Trust

Anyone who likes visiting places of natural beauty and/or historic interest has cause to be grateful to the National Trust. Without it, many such places would probably have vanished by now.

It was in response to the pressures on the countryside posed by the relentless march of Victorian industrialisation that the trust was set up in 1895. Its founders, inspired by the common goals of protecting and conserving Britain's national heritage and widening public access to it, were Sir Robert Hunter, Octavia Hill and Canon Rawnsley: respectively a solicitor, a social reformer and a clergyman. The latter was particularly influential. As a canon of Carlisle Cathedral and vicar of Crosthwaite (near Keswick), he was concerned about threats to the Lake District and had already been active in protecting footpaths and promoting public access to open countryside. After the flooding of Thirlmere in 1879 to create a large reservoir, he became increasingly convinced that the only effective way to guarantee protection was outright ownership of land.

The purpose of the National Trust is to preserve areas of natural beauty and sites of historic interest by acquisition, holding them in trust for the nation and making them available for public access and enjoyment. Some of its properties have been acquired through purchase, but many of the Trust's properties have been donated. Nowadays it is not only one of the biggest landowners in the country, but also one of the most active conservation charities, protecting 581,113 acres (253,176 ha) of land, including 555 miles (892km) of coastline, and over 300 historic properties in England, Wales and Northern Ireland. (There is a separate National Trust for Scotland, which was set up in 1931.)

Furthermore, once a piece of land has come under National Trust ownership, it is difficult for its status to be altered. As a result of parliamentary legislation in 1907, the Trust was given the right to declare its property inalienable, so ensuring that in any subsequent dispute it can appeal directly to parliament.

As it works towards its dual aims of conserving areas of attractive countryside and encouraging greater public access (not easy to reconcile in this age of mass tourism), the Trust provides an excellent service for walkers by creating new concessionary paths and waymarked trails, maintaining stiles and foot bridges and combating the ever-increasing problem of footpath erosion.

For details of membership, contact the National Trust at the address on page 95.

The Ramblers' Association

No organisation works more actively to protect and extend the rights and interests of walkers in the countryside than the Ramblers' Association. Its aims are clear: to foster a greater knowledge, love and care of the countryside; to assist in the protection and enhancement of public rights of way and areas of natural beauty; to work for greater public access to the countryside; and to encourage more people to take up rambling as a healthy, recreational leisure activity.

It was founded in 1935 when, following the setting up of a National Council of Ramblers' Federations in 1931, a number of federations earlier formed in London, Manchester, the Midlands and elsewhere came together to create a more effective pressure group, to deal with such problems as the disappearance and obstruction of footpaths, the prevention of access to open mountain and moorland and increasing hostility from landowners. This was the era of the mass trespasses, when there were sometimes violent

confrontations between ramblers and gamekeepers, especially on the moorlands of the Peak District.

The River Severn near Upton

Since then the Ramblers' Association has played an influential role in preserving and developing the national footpath network, supporting the creation of national parks and encouraging the designation and waymarking of long-distance routes.

Our freedom to walk in the countryside is precarious and requires constant vigilance. As well as the perennial problems of footpaths being illegally obstructed, disappearing through lack of use or extinguished by housing or road construction, new dangers can spring up at any time.

It is to meet such problems and dangers that the Ramblers' Association exists and represents the interests of all walkers. The address to write to for information on the Ramblers' Association and how to become a member is given on page 95.

Walkers and the Law

The average walker in a national park or other popular walking area, armed with the appropriate Ordnance Survey map, reinforced perhaps by a guidebook giving detailed walking instructions, is unlikely to run into legal difficulties, but it is useful to know something about the law relating to public rights of way. The right to walk over certain parts of the countryside has developed over a long period, and how such rights came into being is a complex subject, too lengthy to be discussed here. The following comments are intended simply as a helpful guide, backed up by the Countryside Access Charter, a concise summary of walkers' rights and obligations drawn up by the Countryside Commission (see page 93).

Basically there are two main kinds of public rights of way: footpaths (for walkers only) and bridleways (for walkers, riders on horseback and pedal cyclists). Footpaths and bridleways are shown by broken green lines on Ordnance Survey Explorer maps and broken red lines on Landranger maps. There is also a third category, called byways: chiefly broad tracks (green lanes) or farm roads, which walkers, riders and cyclists have to share, usually only occasionally, with motor vehicles. Many of these public paths have been in existence for hundreds of years and some even originated as prehistoric trackways and have been in constant use for well over 2000 years. Ways known as RUPPs (roads used as public paths) still appear on some maps. The legal definition of such byways is ambiguous and they are gradually being reclassified as footpaths, bridleways or byways.

The term 'right of way' means exactly what it says. It gives right of passage over what, in the vast majority of cases, is private land, and you are required to keep to the line of the path and not stray on to the land on either side. If you inadvertently wander off the right of way – either because of faulty map-reading or because the route is not clearly indicated on the ground – you are technically trespassing and the wisest course is to ask the nearest available person (farmer or fellow walker) to direct you back to the correct route. There are stories about unpleasant confrontations between walkers and farmers at times, but in general most farmers are co-operative when responding to a genuine and polite request for assistance in route-finding.

Obstructions can sometimes be a problem and probably the most common of these is where a path across a field has been ploughed up. It is legal for a farmer to plough up a path provided that he restores it within two weeks, barring exceptionally bad weather. This does not always happen and here the walker is presented with a dilemma: to follow the line of the path, even if this inevitably means treading on crops, or to walk around the edge of the field. The latter course of action often seems the best but this means that you would be trespassing and not keeping to the exact line of the path. In the case of other obstructions which may block a path (illegal fences and locked gates etc), common sense has to be used in order to negotiate them by the easiest method – detour or removal. You should only ever remove as much as is necessary to get through, and if you can easily go round the obstruction without causing any damage, then you should do so. If you have any problems negotiating rights of way, you should report the matter to the rights of way department of

Thatched cottages in Little Comberton

Countryside Access Charter

Your rights of way are:

- public footpaths – on foot only. Sometimes waymarked in yellow
- bridle-ways – on foot, horseback and pedal cycle. Sometimes waymarked in blue
- byways (usually old roads), most 'roads used as public paths' and, of course, public roads – all traffic has the right of way

Use maps, signs and waymarks to check rights of way. Ordnance Survey Explorer and Landranger maps show most public rights of way

On rights of way you can:

- take a pram, pushchair or wheelchair if practicable
- take a dog (on a lead or under close control)
- take a short route round an illegal obstruction or remove it sufficiently to get past

You have a right to go for recreation to:

- public parks and open spaces – on foot
- most commons near older towns and cities – on foot and sometimes on horseback
- private land where the owner has a formal agreement with the local authority

In addition you can use the following by local or established custom or consent, but ask for advice if you are unsure:

- many areas of open country, such as moorland, fell and coastal areas, especially those in the care of the National Trust, and some commons
- some woods and forests, especially those owned by the Forestry Commission
- country parks and picnic sites
- most beaches
- canal towpaths
- some private paths and tracks Consent sometimes extends to horse-riding and cycling

For your information:

- county councils and London boroughs maintain and record rights of way, and register commons
- obstructions, dangerous animals, harassment and misleading signs on rights of way are illegal and you should report them to the county council
- paths across fields can be ploughed, but must normally be reinstated within two weeks
- landowners can require you to leave land to which you have no right of access
- motor vehicles are normally permitted only on roads, byways and some 'roads used as public paths'

the relevant council, which will take action with the landowner concerned.

Apart from rights of way enshrined by law, there are a number of other paths available to walkers. Permissive or concessionary paths have been created where a landowner has given permission for the public to use a particular route across his land. The main problem with these is that, as they have been granted as a concession, there is no legal right to use them and therefore they can be extinguished at any time. In practice, many of these concessionary routes have been established on land owned either by large public bodies such as the Forestry Commission, or by a private one, such as the National Trust, and as these mainly

encourage walkers to use their paths, they are unlikely to be closed unless a change of ownership occurs.

Walkers also have free access to country parks (except where requested to keep away from certain areas for ecological reasons, eg. wildlife protection, woodland regeneration, etc), canal towpaths and most beaches. By custom, though not by right, you are generally free to walk across the open and uncultivated higher land of mountain, moorland and fell, but this varies from area to area and from one season to another – grouse moors, for example, will be out of bounds during the breeding and shooting seasons and some open areas are used as Ministry of Defence firing ranges, for which reason

The imposing 'wool church' at Fairford

in mind before you start. Do not be afraid to abandon your proposed route and return to your starting point in the event of a sudden and unexpected deterioration in the weather.

All the walks described in this book will be safe to do, given due care and respect, even during the winter. Indeed, a crisp, fine winter day often provides perfect walking conditions, with firm ground underfoot and a clarity unique to this time of the year.

The most difficult hazard likely to be encountered is mud, especially when walking along woodland and field paths, farm tracks and bridleways – the latter in particular can often get churned up by cyclists and horses. In summer, an additional difficulty may be narrow and overgrown paths, particularly along the edges of cultivated fields. Neither should constitute a major problem provided that the appropriate footwear is worn.

access will be restricted. In some areas the situation has been clarified as a result of 'access agreements' between the landowners and either the county council or the national park authority, which clearly define when and where you can walk over such open country.

■ Walking Safety

Although the reasonably gentle countryside that is the subject of this book offers no real dangers to walkers at any time of the year, it is still advisable to take sensible precautions and follow certain well-tried guidelines.

Always take with you both warm and waterproof clothing and sufficient food and drink. Wear suitable footwear, such as strong walking boots or shoes that give a good grip over stony ground, on slippery slopes and in muddy conditions. Try to obtain a local weather forecast and bear it

■ Useful Organisations

Council for the Protection of Rural England
128 Southwark Street,
London SE1 0SW
Tel. 020 7981 2800

Countryside Agency
John Dower House, Crescent Place,
Cheltenham, Gloucestershire
GL50 3RA
Tel. 01242 521381

Forestry Commission
Silvan House, 231 Corstorphine Road,
Edinburgh EH12 7AT
Tel. 0131 334 0303

Long Distance Walkers' Association
Bank House, High Street, Wrotham,
Seven Oaks, Kent TN15 7AE
Tel. 01732 883705

National Trust
Membership and general enquiries:
PO Box 39, Warrington WA5 7WD
Tel. 0870 458 4000
West Midlands Regional Office:
Attingham Park, Shrewsbury, Shropshire
Tel. 01743 709343

Ordnance Survey
Romsey Road, Maybush,
Southampton SO16 4GU
Tel. 08456 05 05 05 (Lo-call)

Ramblers' Association
2nd Floor, Camelford House,
87-90 Albert Embankment,
London SE1 7TW
Tel. 020 7339 8500

Tourist Information
Heart of England Tourist Board,
Larkhill Road,
Worcester WR5 2EZ
Tel. 01905 761100

Local tourist information offices:
Banbury: 01295 259855
Broadway: 01386 852937
Burford: 01993 823558
Cheltenham: 01242 522878
Chipping Campden: 01386 841206
Chipping Norton: 01608 644379
Cirencester: 01285 654180
Evesham: 01386 446944
Gloucester: 01452 396572
Kenilworth: 01926 748900
Leamington Spa: 01926 742762
Oxford: 01865 726871
Redditch: 01527 60806
Stow-on-the-Wold: 01451 831082
Stratford-upon-Avon: 0870 160 7930
Stroud: 01453 760960
Tewkesbury: 01684 295027
Warwick: 01926 492212
Witney: 01993 775802
Woodstock: 01993 813276
Worcester: 01905 726311

Youth Hostels Association
Trevelyan House, Dimple Road,
Matlock, Derbyshire
DE4 3YH
Tel. 01629 592600

Ordnance Survey Maps of Shakespeare Country

Shakespeare Country, Vale of Evesham and the Cotswolds are covered by Ordnance Survey 1:50 000 scale ($1\frac{1}{4}$ inches to 1 mile or 2cm to 1km) Landranger map sheets 139, 150, 151, 163 and 164. These all-purpose maps are packed with useful information to help you explore the area. Viewpoints, picnic sites, places of interest and caravan and camping sites are shown, as well as public rights of way information such as footpaths and bridleways.

To examine Shakespeare Country in more detail, and especially if you are planning walks, Ordnance Survey Explorer maps at 1:25 000 scale ($2\frac{1}{2}$ inches to 1 mile or 4cm to 1km) are ideal:

OL45 (The Cotswolds)
169 (Cirencester & Swindon)
180 (Oxford)
190 (Malvern Hills & Bredon Hill)
191 (Banbury, Bicester & Chipping Norton)
205 (Stratford-upon-Avon & Evesham)
206 (Edge Hill & Fenny Compton)
220 (Birmingham)
221 (Coventry & Warwick)

To get to Shakespeare Country use the Ordnance Survey Great Britain OS Travel Map-Route at 1:625 000 (4cm to 25km or 1 inch to 10 miles) scale or Ordnance Survey Road Travel Maps 6 (Wales and West Midlands) and 8 (South East England including London) at 1:250 000 (1cm to 2.5km or 1 inch to 4 miles) scale.

Ordnance Survey maps and guides are available from most booksellers, stationers and newsagents.

www.totalwalking.co.uk

www.totalwalking.co.uk
is the official website of the Jarrold
Pathfinder and Short Walks guides. This
interactive website features a wealth of
information for walkers – from the latest
news on route diversions and advice from
professional walkers to product news, free
sample walks and promotional offers.